ADVANCED
READING
EXPERT

A HIGH-LEVEL READING COURSE for TOP-RANKING EFL Readers

1

ADVANCED
READING
EXPERT *1*

Series Editors	Bin-na Yang, Hae-sung Yang
Project Editors	Jeong-ah Sun, Ji-yeon Lee, In-hye Heo, Hyo-jin Park
Writers	Patrick Ferraro, Keeran Murphy, Paul Nicholas Scherf
Design	Hyunah Song
Editorial Designer	In-sun Lee
Special Thanks to	Seung-pyo Han, Hoe-young Kim, Hey-won Nam

Copyright©2020 by NE Neungyule, Inc.

First Printing 5 January 2020

10th Printing 15 February 2024

ISBN   979-11-253-2932-9

Photo Credits

www.istockphoto.com

www.shutterstock.com

www.dreamstime.com

The <Advanced Reading Expert> series is a two-level reading course for top-ranking EFL readers, with special relevance for senior high school students, as well as some junior high school students. They will acquire not only reading skills but also knowledge of various contemporary and academic topics.

FEATURES

Covering Interesting, Academic Topics: Topics ranging from academic subjects to real world issues are developed in an in-depth, interesting way so that students can advance their thinking ability while developing their reading skills.

Expanding Knowledge: Each unit is composed of two articles under one topic heading. They will help students expand their knowledge of various topics, such as social and academic issues.

Tackling Longer Passages: Interesting and well-developed passages customized for EFL students will help learners to approach longer passages with ease. Summarizing exercises will also help them understand the main points of long passages.

Test-Oriented Questions: Many comprehension checkup questions are similar to iBT TOEFL questions. They will be a stepping stone in preparing students for English tests at school as well as taking official English language tests such as iBT TOEFL.

TO THE **STUDENTS**

Why is reading challenging?

It can be very challenging and sometimes painful for EFL students to read English newspapers, magazines, or books. There are a variety of reasons behind this, including the high level of vocabulary and structure, a lack of background knowledge on the topic, and insufficient reading skills.

Become an expert reader with the <Advanced Reading Expert> series!

The <Advanced Reading Expert> series is a two-level reading course designed to raise your reading ability to a higher level. There are four reading strategies you need to focus on to improve your reading ability.

1. Vocabulary Skills

When you run into an unfamiliar word, try to continue reading. A couple of unfamiliar words usually won't prevent you from gaining a general understanding of a passage. If you think they are a barrier to further reading, use context clues. If that does not provide enough information, it may be necessary to use your Word Book or look up the problem word in the dictionary.

2. Paragraph Approach

A passage is a collection of paragraphs: The main point of each paragraph is organized into the main idea of the passage. When you read a passage, try not to just focus on the meaning of each sentence: Keep asking yourself, "What is the main point of this paragraph?" Questions on both the main point of a paragraph and the summary exercises will help you stay focused.

3. Understanding Longer Passages

Even high-level EFL readers sometimes find it quite challenging to read and understand long passages. They must rely on reading skills such as scanning, skimming, understanding the structure of the passage, etc. Reading comprehension questions and summary exercises cover these reading skills.

4. Knowledge of the Topic

When reading any language, a lack of background knowledge can prevent you from understanding the topic. The <Advanced Reading Expert> series covers a variety of topics, including academic subjects, social issues, world culture, etc. If you are not familiar with the topic in question, try to search for relevant information in books or on the Internet.

TO THE **TEACHER**

Series Overview

\<Advanced Reading Expert\> is a high-level reading course written by professional writers and EFL teachers who have years of experience in teaching EFL students. It is simple to use in the classroom and interesting enough to attract students' attention. Each level is composed of 16 units and each unit has two readings.

Each unit contains the following sections:

Readings & Comprehension Checkups

There are two readings for every topic. A reading is followed by comprehension checkup questions. These activities are intended to allow students to practice various reading skills such as identifying the main idea, understanding specific details, etc.

Summary

This section is useful for a variety of purposes. Have the students complete the summary without referring to the reading first. This tests whether students understand the text as a whole.

Word Check

After reading and answering the questions, students can check the key vocabulary in the Word Check section.

Audio Recording

Students can listen to an audio recording of each passage using the MP3 files that can be downloaded from our homepage (www.nebooks.co.kr).

Word Review Test

Expanding their vocabulary is important for EFL readers. Therefore, they need to review unfamiliar words. This section is intended to test their vocabulary every four units.

TABLE OF **CONTENTS**

Much of the food that is available today is full of chemicals and processed substances. Called "additives," they are used to give food more flavor and better texture and to increase its shelf life. However, some of the most common additives have been shown to cause serious health problems.

5   Aspartame, one of the most common food additives, is an artificial sweetener used in foods that are labeled "diet" and "sugar free." Studies have linked it to various types of cancer, diabetes, anxiety, and many other diseases and conditions. It is found in a wide variety of foods: diet and sugar-free soft drinks, sugar-free gum and breath mints, various desserts, toothpaste, and even chewable vitamins!

10   Another dangerous artificial sweetener is high fructose corn syrup (HFCS). It increases levels of LDL, or "bad" cholesterol, damages bodily tissues, and causes people to gain weight. Amazingly, because it is used in nearly all processed foods, it has become one of the main sources of calories for many people.

    Monosodium glutamate, or MSG, is used to enhance the flavor of soups, salad
15 dressings, snacks, frozen foods, and more. Because it turns off the brain's neurological pathways that make you feel full, it leads many people to overeat. MSG also seriously damages cells, and studies have linked regular consumption of the additive to depression, eye damage, fatigue, and headaches.

    Finally, trans fat, which is found in fast food, margarine, and other processed foods,
20 also enhances food's natural flavor. However, not only does it increase levels of LDL cholesterol, but it also decreases levels of HDL, or "good" cholesterol. It has been linked to all kinds of health problems, from diabetes to heart disease. In fact, it is considered so dangerous that it is now either highly restricted or banned in countries such as Denmark, Iceland, and Sweden.

25   Unfortunately, food additives have become so common that they can be hard to avoid. However, there are things you can do to start eating healthier. Instead of eating fast food and processed foods, eat home cooked meals as often as you can. And when you buy groceries, remember to read the food labels, which list the ingredients and any
30 additives that the food contains. Finally, buy as many organic products as you can. The more often you eat natural, whole foods, the healthier you will be!

Choose the correct words for the blanks from the highlighted words in the passage.

1. the act of eating or drinking: _____
2. to improve the quality of sth: _____
3. limited or controlled to reduce availability: _____
4. having been preserved or changed chemically: _____

1 What is the best title for the passage?
   a. How Food Additives Can Be Avoided
   b. What Additives Do in Processed Foods
   c. How Food Additives Are Harming Your Health
   d. Why Additives Are Used Excessively in Processed Foods

2 Write the best answer choice for the following explanation.

aspartame	high fructose corn syrup	MSG	trans fat

   a. It prevents people from feeling full, leading them to excessive eating. _____
   b. As the main source of calories, it causes people to put on weight. _____
   c. It is found in various sugar-free products and causes many diseases. _____

3 Which is NOT true about trans fat according to the passage?
   a. It is found in margarine and fast or processed foods.
   b. It is a food additive made of natural ingredients.
   c. It increases LDL cholesterol levels while decreasing HDL levels.
   d. It is regulated or prohibited in some countries.

4 According to paragraph 6, what are three ways to eat healthy?

   _____

SUMMARY

5 Use the words in the box to fill in the blanks.

artificial	damages	weight	natural	full	chemicals	texture

Dangerous Food Additives

Aspartame	High fructose corn syrup
▪ _____ sweetener ▪ used in "diet" and "sugar-free" foods ▪ linked to cancer and diabetes, and other diseases	▪ used in almost all processed foods ▪ increases "bad" cholesterol ▪ makes people gain _____
MSG	**Trans fat**
▪ used to enhance the flavor of food ▪ prevents one from feeling _____ ▪ linked to depression, fatigue, and more	▪ enhances food's _____ flavor ▪ linked to many health problems ▪ banned in several countries

Why do people drink soda? It's probably because they think it tastes good. But lately the soft drink market has been flooded with products that claim to have an effect beyond taste. Energy drinks are one of these newcomers on the soft drink scene.
5 As their name implies, they claim to supply an energy boost. They're designed for students, athletes, and anyone else who wants an extra energy kick. But there are worries about the true effect they can have on the body.

Energy drinks provide physical and mental stimulation over a short period of time.
10 But this is not because energy drinks contain a variety of vitamins and health additives. The real effect drinkers feel comes from the simple combination of sugar and caffeine. A single energy drink typically contains more than twice as much caffeine as a can of soda. Caffeine inhibits the production of adenosine, which promotes sleep, and increases adrenaline and dopamine, which can make a person feel alert.

15 The risks of consuming energy drinks are, therefore, roughly the same as those of drinking coffee. Some people complain of an increase in their heart rate, feelings of anxiety, and trouble sleeping. And as caffeine has an addictive quality, energy drink consumers may find it difficult to limit themselves to the recommended maximum of 500 ml per day as indicated on the product labels of many of the large energy drink
20 manufacturers.

Unlike sports drinks, which assist in rehydrating the body during physical exercise, energy drinks actually act as a *diuretic, thereby decreasing the amount of water retained in one's body. It is easy to see, therefore, that consuming energy drinks during prolonged periods of exercise can be dangerous. The potential hazards, however, go beyond the risk
25 of dehydration. Some energy drinks also contain ephedrine, a stimulant often used in diet pills that has been linked to heart problems, along with other ingredients whose effects are not yet fully understood.

When used in moderation, energy drinks can be a safe source of stimulation for people who are feeling listless. It is important, however, to understand exactly what we
30 are putting into our bodies and the effects it may have.

*diuretic: a substance that causes the body to lose liquids

Choose the correct words for the blanks from the highlighted words in the passage.

1. to restrain or hold back: _____
2. a potential danger or risk: _____
3. a lack of water in the body: _____
4. a substance added in small amounts to sth: _____

1 What is the main idea of the passage?

    a. Energy drinks are more beneficial than other soft drinks.

    b. Energy drinks provide extra energy but can be dangerous.

    c. The ingredients in energy drinks have no nutritional value.

    d. Energy drinks have no effect on people who need more energy.

2 Who do energy drink producers target?

    _____

3 Which is NOT mentioned as a risk of energy drinks?

    a. an increased heart rate

    b. muscle pain

    c. trouble sleeping

    d. dehydration

4 Which is closest in meaning to listless?

    a. uneasy   b. nervous   c. cheerless   d. depressed

5 Which is NOT true about energy drinks according to the passage?

    a. They quickly provide physical and mental stimulation.

    b. There are concerns about their influence on the body.

    c. They contain half the recommended amount of caffeine.

    d. They decrease the amount of water in the body.

SUMMARY

6 Match each main point to the correct paragraph in the passage.

    a. Paragraph 1 •   • ① Energy drinks and coffee have similar adverse effects.

    b. Paragraph 2 •   • ② Energy drinks are popular but possibly harmful.

    c. Paragraph 3 •   • ③ Energy drinks use sugar and caffeine to provide a kick.

    d. Paragraph 4 •   • ④ We should be aware of the effects of energy drinks before drinking them.

    e. Paragraph 5 •   • ⑤ Energy drinks can cause dehydration and heart problems.

I ndividuals ought to focus on what they're good at. For example, great actors should dedicate their time to filming movies; it would be a waste of their talent not to. But people can be skilled at other things as well. For instance, let's say that an actor is
5 particularly good at mowing lawns. Does that mean that he should mow the huge lawn around his mansion by himself? Looking at the economic concepts of absolute advantage, opportunity cost and comparative advantage may help us answer this question.

Suppose the actor can mow his lawn in four hours and that it would take a teenage boy
10 from his neighborhood eight hours to do the same job. If we compare their productivity, economists would say that the actor has an absolute advantage over the teenager because he would invest half the input to get the same result. In other words, the actor is more efficient when considering the quantity of time required to do the job. However, the value of his time should also be taken into account.

15 During those four hours, the actor could film a television commercial and make $50,000. These potential earnings are the actor's opportunity cost of choosing to mow his lawn instead of filming the commercial. The concept of opportunity cost refers to what we lose when we decide on a certain action. It should be considered when determining whether doing something is worth the loss associated with the action. If the teenager
20 would only earn $80 working for eight hours at a fast food restaurant instead, he would lose much less than the actor would.

This comparison of opportunity cost is the key to determining who should mow the lawn. This is how comparative advantage is calculated. According to this concept, whoever has the lower opportunity cost has a comparative advantage and should perform
25 the action. In this case, that would be the teenager, as long as he makes more than $80 and it costs the actor less than $50,000.

Both the teenager and actor would be better off if the actor hired the boy to mow his lawn while he filmed the commercial. Similarly, governments consider opportunity cost and comparative advantage when looking at the production of various countries
30 to determine optimal gains from trade. By doing this, they ensure that every country benefits from trading goods with other countries.

WORD
CHECK

Choose the correct words for the blanks from the highlighted words in the passage.

1. the best possible: _____
2. connected or related to sth else: _____
3. an extremely large and beautiful house: _____
4. to cut grass, especially with tools or machines: _____

1 What is the best title for the passage?
   a. Decision Making Based on Economic Concepts
   b. For Future Economists: Economical Ways of Thinking
   c. Understanding the Most Important Economic Concepts in Trading
   d. A Comparison between Absolute Advantage and Comparative Advantage

2 Which is closest in meaning to <u>taken into account</u>?
   a. implied   b. valued   c. accounted for   d. considered

3 What does the concept of opportunity cost refer to according to paragraph 3?

   _____

4 According to paragraph 4, comparative advantage is the ability to produce goods

   _____.

   a. in shorter time than another
   b. using fewer inputs than another
   c. of the best quality faster than another
   d. at a lower opportunity cost than another

5 Who best understands the economic concepts mentioned in the passage?
   a. Irene: The boy has an absolute advantage because it takes him more time to mow the
        lawn than the actor.
   b. Betty: If the actor decides to mow the lawn instead of filming the commercial, his
        opportunity cost is what he earns by mowing the lawn.
   c. Alex: The boy has a comparative advantage in mowing the lawn because his
        opportunity cost is less than the actor's.
   d. James: The actor should film the commercial because he has a comparative advantage
        in mowing the lawn.

SUMMARY

6 Use the words in the box to fill in the blanks.

| lower   decide   higher   absolute   lose   gain   calculate |

Applying economic concepts can help _____ whether an actor or a teenage boy
should mow a lawn. If the actor could do it in half the time it would take the
teenager, he would have a(n) _____ advantage. However, his opportunity cost
would be much _____, since he could earn $50,000 filming a commercial
instead, while the boy could only earn $80 elsewhere during this time. Thus, the
teenager has a comparative advantage and should mow the lawn because he would
_____ much less by performing this task.

Demarketing

Marketing can be defined as the act of creating, maintaining and expanding a demand for a specific product or service. Certain scenarios exist, however, in which organizations seek to discourage this same demand. In these cases, a process known as "demarketing" is employed.

5 Generally speaking, demarketing can be broken down into three categories, the first of which is known as general demarketing. This occurs when a product is demarketed to all users, often in times of shortage, when governments seek to persuade citizens to limit their consumption of a resource such as gasoline or electricity. It is also implemented when a product is deemed to be a risk to public health.

10 Selective demarketing, on the other hand, is aimed at a specific segment of the population. Businesses will generally use selective demarketing on a group of customers that has proven to be less profitable. These fringe users are discouraged, and marketing resources are focused on a more profitable core. Some banks, for example, offer specialized services for customers with large balances, while low profit customers must 15 queue up for a turn at the ATM.

The third category, ostensible demarketing, is exemplified by situations in which a business withholds the availability of a product in order to heighten its appeal. This type of demarketing is often applied to high-end toys during the Christmas season, as the difficulties consumers face in purchasing the item increase its value in their eyes. Therefore, 20 demand is actually raised, rather than lowered.

Some companies that are seeking to create an upscale image demarket their products by limiting the scope of their advertising. ■ A jewelry company might advertise only in a handful of magazines, giving their products the illusion of exclusivity. ■ Similarly, other companies demarket by limiting the scope of their distribution, such as a liquor 25 manufacturer that only sells their whiskey in expensive bars. ■ Tobacco companies use such labels to educate current users while making themselves seem more compassionate. ■ Through these methods, companies can create a luxurious brand image or improve their corporate image.

To look at demarketing as nothing more than the opposite of marketing would be a 30 gross oversimplification. It is a nuanced business strategy that can be employed in a variety of situations to help control the tides of public demand.

---

1 The word employ in the passage is closest in meaning to

  ⓐ declare   ⓑ implement   ⓒ demonstrate   ⓓ approve

2 Based on paragraph 2, the following can be inferred as examples of general demarketing EXCEPT

ⓐ a national campaign to save energy

ⓑ an advertisement to inform the public about the danger of heavy drinking

ⓒ a video made by the government to explain a water shortage

ⓓ a high-priced brand's policy to limit the number of items a customer can buy

3 According to paragraph 3, the selective demarketing strategies banks use are _____.

ⓐ focusing more on fringe users

ⓑ offering customized services to customers with large balances

ⓒ encouraging the bank users to use ATMs by themselves

ⓓ asking customers with low balances to sign up for new services

4 Why does the author mention high-end toys in paragraph 4?

ⓐ to describe the negative consequences of ostensible demarketing

ⓑ to show how the law of supply and demand works in a real economy

ⓒ to give an example of demarketing used to increase a product's value

ⓓ to explain how unproductive it is to use ostensible demarketing to customers

5 Look at the four squares [■] that indicate where the following sentence could be added to the passage.

Another approach is the use of warning labels outlining health risks associated with a product.

Where would the sentence best fit?

6 Directions   Complete the table by matching the phrases below. Select the appropriate phrases from the answer choices and match them to each category which they relate. TWO of the answer choices should NOT be used.

Answer Choices
ⓐ Gives products an image that makes them seem exclusive or desirable
ⓑ Attempts to discourage certain customers in favor of more profitable ones
ⓒ Draws a comparison between a product and its less popular competition
ⓓ Used to keep consumers from purchasing products that are scarce
ⓔ Allows consumers to locate products that are sometimes hard to find
ⓕ Can serve to protect the public from products that are bad for their health
ⓖ Results in an increase in product demand rather than a decrease

General Demarketing:	Selective Demarketing:	Ostensible Demarketing:

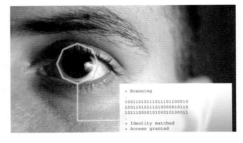

> Scanning
1001101011101100010
1001101011101000010110
1011100001010002100011

> Identity matched
> Access granted

You might forget your password, you could misplace your keys, but you'll never leave home without yourself. Hailed as a safer alternative to passcodes, high-tech biometric **authentication**
5 systems are beginning to replace traditional security measures.

Biometric systems authenticate the identity of individuals by recognizing their unique physical or behavioral traits. These systems are automated, highly accurate, and don't take a lot of time or training to use. Their advantage over traditional security
10 systems is that they don't rely on components that can be lost or easily stolen.

The first step in utilizing a biometric authentication system is **enrollment**. This involves the use of a sensor to detect and compile basic biometric information on each individual who will use the system. Storage occurs next as the information is **converted** into mathematical algorithms and entered into a computer database. The final step is
15 comparison. Relevant biometric traits are scanned, and the results are compared using a software program, with the information stored in the database. If they match, the subject's identity has been authenticated and access is granted.

There are a variety of biometric analyses that can confirm an individual's identity. Handwriting is one such option. Subjects write a word on a touch pad, and the system
20 analyzes such diverse factors as speed, rhythm, pressure of writing, and the angle of the pen. Iris scanning is another popular form of biometric analysis. After the system's camera takes a picture of the eye, it authenticates the individual by measuring and analyzing the pupil, iris, eyelid, and eyelashes using near-infrared light. Another unique physical **attribute** utilized in biometrics is vein geometry. This system analyzes the shape and
25 location of the vein structure using a camera with infrared light.

Biometrics offers a more reliable means of identification than traditional **security** systems. There are, however, _____ (A) _____. Once the biometric data has been captured by a system, it can potentially be forwarded to other locations and put to many different uses without the owner's consent. If tech-savvy thieves can reproduce
30 users' biometric IDs, the users may be faced with a lifelong problem, since personal traits can't be changed or reset. These issues will have to be addressed if biometrics is to become an everyday fixture in our lives.

WORD CHECK

Choose the correct words for the blanks from the highlighted words in the passage.

1. a feature or trait of sb or sth: _____
2. to change sth into a different form: _____
3. the act of joining or registering for sth: _____
4. the act of verifying the credibility of sth: _____

1 What is the passage mainly about?

    a. a revolutionary way of confirming our identities

    b. a new technology for protecting personal identity

    c. an effective method of analyzing personal data banks

    d. a biometric program that uses physical traits to analyze personalities

2 Put the following steps of biometric systems in order.

    a. allowing the individual access

    b. using sensors to record biometric data

    c. storing biometric information in a computer

    d. comparing scanned traits with those stored in a computer

3 Complete the following chart with information from the passage.

Biometric System	Personal Traits
Handwriting	*speed, rhythm, pressure of writing, and the angle of the pen*
Iris scanning	(1)
Vein geometry	(2)

4 What is the best expression for blank (A)?

    a. some cost problems

    b. some privacy concerns

    c. occasional technical problems

    d. more reliable identification systems

5 Which is NOT true about biometric authentication systems according to the passage?

    a. No passcodes are needed.

    b. They are based on an individual's physical or behavioral traits.

    c. They don't require a lot of time.

    d. Personal traits used for authentication cannot be duplicated.

SUMMARY

6 Match each topic to the correct paragraph in the passage.

    a. Paragraph 1 •   • ① various methods of confirming a user's identity

    b. Paragraph 2 •   • ② the merits of biometric systems

    c. Paragraph 3 •   • ③ a high-tech security system

    d. Paragraph 4 •   • ④ how biometric authentication systems work

    e. Paragraph 5 •   • ⑤ potential problems with biometric authentication systems

King Harald Bluetooth of Denmark made history by uniting his kingdom with Norway in the tenth century. Hundreds of years later, a new Bluetooth is making its own reputation by bringing together electronic devices through wireless technology.

5 Named in honor of King Harald, Bluetooth technology was developed by Ericsson, a Swedish telecommunications company, as a means of eliminating cumbersome cable connections between portable electronic devices, such as laptops, mobile phones, and digital cameras. Data normally shared through these cables is instead communicated

10 through the medium of radio waves. These waves can be transmitted up to distances of 10 m, seeking out and connecting with other wireless devices. Bluetooth isn't a heavy power consumer, it doesn't require any expensive hardware, and it sets up networks quickly and easily.

There are a myriad of conveniences we can enjoy thanks to Bluetooth: We can talk

15 on our mobile phones through wireless headsets while walking or driving; keyboards and mouses can be connected to our computers without wires, allowing for more flexibility and freedom of movement while we're confined to our desks; and we can transfer music files to our iPods with ease or effortlessly download photos from our digital cameras. Bluetooth technology is also a factor in the facilitation of social networking, allowing

20 strangers to exchange personal profiles, messages, or business cards by sensing all other Bluetooth-enabled devices in range and automatically establishing temporary networks.

However, the ease with which Bluetooth creates connections can also be the source of some security concerns. Bluejacking is the practice of sending anonymous text messages that resemble system-generated warnings. It's a harmless prank but can be distressing to

25 inexperienced users. Bluesnarfing is a more critical security threat. If hackers manage to covertly create a connection through Bluetooth, they can take control of your wireless device and use it as a vehicle for transmitting viruses.

Practices that can prevent this type of threat include turning off Bluetooth when your device is not in use and hiding your device from unknown Bluetooth users by

30 switching off the discovery mode. Firewalls and anti-virus software can also be installed for enhanced safety. Despite these security challenges, Bluetooth continues to reign as the industry standard for wireless technology, making it easier than ever to bring together all our portable electronic devices.

WORD CHECK

Choose the correct words for the blanks from the highlighted words in the passage.

1. too many to count: _____
2. a practical joke or trick: _____
3. having no known name: _____
4. difficult to use or handle: _____

1 What is the best title for the passage?
   a. Bluetooth: A Necessity for IT Advancement
   b. Bluetooth: The Expansion of Media Production
   c. Bluetooth: The New King of Wireless Technology
   d. Bluetooth: A Digital Device for Multi-user Communication

2 According to the passage, with Bluetooth technology, we can _____.
   a. easily upgrade portable device systems
   b. improve the storage capacity of personal computers
   c. transmit a massive amount of information at a faster speed
   d. connect electronic devices and exchange information over radio waves

3 Bluejacking can be distressing to users by _____.

4 Which is closest in meaning to <u>covertly</u>?
   a. secretly   b. broadly   c. illegally   d. continuously

5 Which of the following is NOT true according to the passage?
   a. Special hardware is necessary to use Bluetooth.
   b. Bluetooth creates temporary networks between users in range.
   c. Bluetooth can threaten individual privacy.
   d. The installation of firewalls is recommended to make using Bluetooth more secure.

SUMMARY

6 Use the words in the box to fill in the blanks.

| radio | waves | automatic | portable | wireless | security | ease | freedom |

Developed by Ericsson, Bluetooth brings together different electronic devices through _____ technology. It works by sending data through _____ as opposed to using cables. Because of Bluetooth, users have more _____ to enjoy various devices, download files, and effortlessly exchange information with others. However, this _____ of use makes it possible for hackers to use Bluetooth for illegal purposes.

Minimalism is a style of art that exists free of outside influences and deeper meanings. It is unconcerned with social issues or the artist's emotions, focusing instead on the creation of
5 beauty by using a minimum of components. The term minimalism was first used in the United States in 1929 to describe an exhibit by the artist John Graham. Minimalism became a household word in the 1960s when it was resurrected to describe what would eventually become known as the minimalist movement.

10   The movement was focused on precision, with roots in mathematics and geometry. The artwork featured repetitive patterns of simple colors, with no hidden themes or meanings. The minimalists felt complex compositions, deep symbolism, and social themes diminished the experience of appreciating the object itself. It was this appreciation that minimalists focused on. Their art was not self-expression; it was pure visual effect. They
15 didn't want viewers to be distracted by the need to figure it out.

      The term minimalism can be used to describe anything that is created with a similar raw aesthetic, and it has been applied to a wide range of mediums, including music, design, architecture, and literature. In music, minimalism features repetitive sounds and a steady beat. Minimalist design relies on basic shapes and clean lines. Minimalist
20 architecture also makes the most of little decoration, stressing the importance of empty spaces and subscribing to the credo of "less is more." And literary minimalism uses words economically, describing only the basic outlines of a situation and featuring characters who are ordinary people living ordinary lives.

      Not surprisingly, minimalism has been subjected to a flood of criticism. It has been
25 dismissed as being less than true art or as being heartless and mechanical. Minimalists essentially forced the art world to confront a fundamental question: When meaning and motives are removed from art, what is left behind? Critics would likely say it was "
_____(A)_____." Proponents of minimalism, on the other hand, might claim that the answer is "_____(B)_____." Regardless of personal opinions about its artistic merit,
30 there is little doubt that minimalism has had a significant impact on the postmodern art scene.

WORD
CHECK

Choose the correct words for the blanks from the highlighted words in the passage.
1. a set of beliefs: _____
2. to choose not to consider or accept sth: _____
3. the mathematics of points, lines, and surfaces: _____
4. a philosophical view in matters of artistic beauty: _____

1 **What is the best title for the passage?**
   a. Minimalism: When Less Is More
   b. Minimalism: Focusing on Artists' Emotions
   c. Minimalism: What Lies beneath Modern Art
   d. Minimalism: The Harmony between Art and Reality

2 **Which is closest in meaning to** **diminished?**
   a. captured   b. lessened   c. implied   d. strengthened

3 **Which statement would a minimalist be MOST likely to make?**
   a. I focused on the unity of color in every space.
   b. The distinctive feature of my work is a lack of decoration.
   c. I tried to change the sound and beat a lot to express the theme.
   d. I concentrated on describing the characters in my book in detail.

4 **What is the best pair for blanks (A) and (B)?**

(A)		(B)
a. less emotional art	—	more creative art
b. mechanical repetition	—	abstract beauty
c. oversimplification of theme	—	self-centered art
d. a soulless collection of colors and lines	—	pure beauty

5 **Which is true about minimalism according to the passage?**
   a. The term was first introduced in the 1960s.
   b. It represents beauty by using few components.
   c. Its purpose is to express the artist's feelings.
   d. It focuses on understanding underlying meanings.

SUMMARY

6 **Use the words in the box to fill in the blanks.**

> unconcerned influenced minimum variety appreciating describing cold

Minimalism is a style of art _____ with external factors. Instead, it concentrates on producing beauty with a _____ of components. Minimalist artists want viewers to focus on _____ the object itself rather than trying to understand hidden themes. However, it has been criticized as too _____ and mechanical. Nevertheless, its supporters can point to its important place in postmodern art.

Op Art

The twentieth century witnessed the creation of many innovative and experimental disciplines in the visual arts. Among them was what came to be known as "op art," or "optical art." Found primarily in paintings, op art utilizes certain abstract geometric patterns and color contrasts to create a sense of movement in the mind of the observer. By tricking the
5   eye with such optical illusions, op art explores the relationship between the act of seeing and the act of perceiving what is seen.

Though its foundations were laid as far back as the 1920s and artists have been experimenting with it ever since then, op art did not gain much recognition until the mid-1960s. An exhibition of international op artists in New York City in 1965 called *The*
10 *Responsive Eye* was much celebrated by the public. Art critics were less impressed, but the popularity of op art continued to grow during the remainder of the decade.

The dominant quality of op-art paintings is that the images appear to be moving or vibrating. Many early op-art works were done primarily in black and white, and they relied on geometric patterns and the repetition of lines to give a two-dimensional picture a sense
15 of depth, shape, and movement. Such techniques could even create the illusion of color. Later paintings that were done in color seemed to flicker or vibrate in the viewer's eye as a result of the contrast generated when opposing colors were placed close together.

Even though op-art paintings could create the illusion of a third dimension, it was often difficult to ascertain which aspects of the picture were in the background and which
20 occupied the foreground. In fact, as another type of simulated movement, the foreground and background might appear to be continuously switching places.

The op-art movement was truly an international one. ■ Two of the most recognized artists in the discipline were Bridget Riley of England, whose pieces were mostly black and white, and the Hungarian Victor Vasarely, who often painted in color. ■ Thanks to the
25 recognition received by these artists, op art's popularity skyrocketed in the 1960s, and it began to appear in graphic designs and fabrics. ■ Demand for op art faded with the start of a new decade, but artists continue to experiment with it today, and exhibitions are held regularly. ■

1   According to paragraph 2, which is true about the development of op art?

ⓐ It began in the early 1960s.

ⓑ It was abandoned in 1965.

ⓒ It was largely unrecognized by the public for years.

ⓓ It took place primarily in New York City.

2 Op-art painting is likely to appear to have a third dimension because

    ⓐ it contains no underlying symbolic themes.

    ⓑ it uses a variety of colors and compositions.

    ⓒ the effective use of empty space makes it possible.

    ⓓ geometric patterns and line repetition can trick the eyes.

3 Why does the author mention opposing colors in paragraph 3?

    ⓐ to contrast two different styles of op art

    ⓑ to explain how geometric patterns were used

    ⓒ to describe what makes op art two-dimensional

    ⓓ to present a technique for simulating movement

4 The word ascertain in the passage is closest in meaning to

    ⓐ imitate   ⓑ predict   ⓒ replace   ⓓ determine

5 Look at the four squares [■] that indicate where the following sentence could be added to the passage.

For example, the women's fashion industry incorporated the black-and-white style made famous by Riley.

Where would the sentence best fit?

6   Directions   An introductory sentence for a brief summary of the passage is provided below. Complete the summary by selecting the THREE answer choices that express the most important ideas in the passage.

Op art was one of the many innovative art styles created in the twentieth century.

    ⓐ Op art became popular with the public in the late 1960s after decades of experimentation.

    ⓑ *The Responsive Eye* exhibition introduced op art to the mainstream art community.

    ⓒ Op artists used geometric patterns, line repetition, and opposing colors to give a sense of depth, shape, and movement to their paintings.

    ⓓ It was easy to distinguish between the foreground and background in op-art paintings.

    ⓔ Bridget Riley, the most famous op artist, often used black and white.

    ⓕ Bridget Riley and Victor Vasarely contributed to op art's popularity and its expansion into various areas.

WORD REVIEW TEST

[1~4] Choose the word that is closest in meaning to the underlined one.

1. The taste of a bottle of wine is <u>determined</u> by its age.
   - a. defined
   - b. conveyed
   - c. decided
   - d. developed

2. Although it looks like a real flower, it is actually <u>artificial</u>.
   - a. cultivated
   - b. man-made
   - c. superficial
   - d. planted

3. The university received $200,000 from an <u>anonymous</u> donor.
   - a. generous
   - b. dominant
   - c. significant
   - d. unnamed

4. That's only a <u>temporary</u> measure, not the fundamental solution for the problem.
   - a. diverse
   - b. simple
   - c. common
   - d. momentary

[5~8] Connect each phrase in column B with its matching verb in column A.

A	B
5. queue up •	• a. information
6. trade •	• b. at the bus stop
7. compile •	• c. with foreign countries
8. hold •	• d. an exhibition

[9~12] Choose the best word to complete each sentence. (Change the form if needed.)

duplicate	attribute	inhibit	organic	discipline	commercial	fringe

9. One of the _____ of a good teacher is patience.

10. The church _____ its people from smoking and drinking.

11. Movie theaters sometimes show many _____ before a film.

12. _____ food is good for the health of both humans and the environment.

[13~16] Choose the correct word for each definition.

comparative	credo	flicker	fixture	calculate	additive	commodity

13. product that can be sold for a profit:

14. a substance that is added to food to improve its taste or appearance:

15. to move back and forth quickly and repeatedly:

16. to figure out the amount or number of something:

[17~22] Choose the best word to complete each sentence.

17. Hotel rates _____ for the holidays.
     a. overlooked   b. charged   c. skyrocketed   d. confronted

18. His ideas were _____ by the professor as being unrealistic.
     a. hailed   b. impressed   c. enhanced   d. dismissed

19. It was deeply _____ for him to see his wife in such pain.
     a. hesitant   b. distressing   c. distinctive   d. inexperienced

20. Wool _____ heat better than cotton.
     a. integrates   b. retains   c. abandons   d. implements

21. Fifteen divided by four gives you a _____ of 3.
     a. fringe   b. shortage   c. remainder   d. quota

22. Henry is _____ to bed due to the car accident.
     a. linked   b. committed   c. opposed   d. confined

[23~25] Circle the odd one out in each group.

23. boost   enrich   heighten   resurrect
24. inhibit   withhold   reign   restrain
25. basic   essential   ostensible   fundamental

[26] Read and write the right number of the correct definition for each sentence.

> **address** *v.* **1.** to put an address on (an envelope, package etc): *That letter was addressed to me.* **2.** to give a speech to a large group of people: *He addressed an audience of 10,000 supporters.* **3.** to deal with (a problem etc): *Your essay does not address the real issues.*

a. The President has been asked to address the assembly. _____
b. The article addresses the problems of child obesity. _____

Most of us have heard the expression "you are what you eat." According to the creator of the macrobiotic diet, however, food influences our lives to a much greater degree than the wisdom of that saying suggests. Although its name stems from the Greek words "macro" (long) and "bios" (life), the macrobiotic diet isn't simply designed
5 to extend lifespans. It also aims to make people happier and give them a greater sense of well-being.

The diet is the creation of Japanese philosopher George Ohsawa, who borrowed the twin principles of Yin and Yang from Taoism to formulate his macrobiotic diet. Yin foods are usually water-based, lighter, refreshing, and high in potassium. Yang foods are more
10 solid, and although they are easy to digest, they provide robust energy. Just as Taoism encourages practitioners to balance their lives between the forces of Yin and Yang, the macrobiotic diet proposes consuming foods in a manner that strikes a similar balance. Owing to the cycles of nature, different foods are recommended at different times of the year and even different times of the day.

15 Preferred foods include whole grains, brown rice, cereals, vegetables, fruits, and fish. The macrobiotic diet recommends that its followers consume locally grown organic foods rather than processed or imported items. It even suggests that meals be prepared by traditional methods rather than modern ones using electric stoves or microwaves. Finally, the macrobiotic diet teaches us not to waste any of the ingredients during the
20 preparation of meals.

Research into the macrobiotic diet indicates that because of its low-fat and high-fiber content, it benefits people by reducing cholesterol, working toward the prevention of heart disease, reducing the risk of cancer, assisting with weight management, and strengthening the immune system. Critics, on the other hand, point out that there is no
25 convincing scientific proof to the extravagant claims that the macrobiotic diet can help cure those stricken with serious diseases like cancer. They also voice concerns that the diet is too restrictive, lacking protein, iron, calcium, and vitamin B12.

The macrobiotic diet does, however, remind us of the important link between living well and eating well. As our lives become
30 busier and more stressful, we might all benefit from rediscovering traditional approaches to what we eat and how we eat it.

WORD
CHECK

Choose the correct words for the blanks from the highlighted words in the passage.

1. the length of time sb lives: _____
2. limiting one's choices: _____
3. to devise or develop sth as a system: _____
4. sb who follows and practices a set of beliefs: _____

1   What is the best title for the passage?
   a. Taoism: Its Origin and Growth
   b. The Pros and Cons of Organic Diets
   c. A Return to Traditional Cooking Methods
   d. Macrobiotic Diet: Not Only Living Long but Also Living Well

2   What do Taoism and the macrobiotic diet have in common according to paragraph 2?

_____

3   Which is NOT mentioned as a benefit of the macrobiotic diet?
   a. lowering cholesterol
   b. tackling weight problems and obesity
   c. helping the immune system
   d. providing in sufficient proteins and vitamins

4   Which is closest in meaning to extravagant?
   a. accurate   b. objective   c. excessive   d. extraordinary

5   Which is true about the macrobiotic diet according to the passage?
   a. It suggests obtaining essential nutrients from food with high calories.
   b. It recommends eating organic food rather than processed food.
   c. It is particularly appropriate for the elderly.
   d. It advocates the fast preparation of meals.

SUMMARY

6   Use the words in the box to fill in the blanks.

| cycle | immune | restrictive | extend | energy | traditional | cholesterol |

The purpose of the macrobiotic diet is to _____ people's lifespans, make them happier and increase their sense of well-being. Created by a Japanese philosopher, it features a balance of light foods that are high in potassium and solid foods that provide _____. Brown rice, vegetables and fish are commonly included, and people following a macrobiotic diet are encouraged to eat local food and use _____ cooking methods. Critics say the diet is too _____, but it reminds us to pay attention to what we eat.

What if we could live in a world without medicine? What if human beings had the ability to heal themselves with the power of their own minds? It may sound like science fiction, but a real life therapy method called "biofeedback" is training people to
5 use their brains to control what ails their bodies.

Biofeedback therapists train patients to control bodily responses, such as changes in their blood pressure and brain activity that are usually considered to be involuntary. Sometimes it is used to treat specific problems. A physical therapist might train stroke victims to regain proper
10 use of their muscles, a psychologist can help people learn how to relax, and a medical specialist might teach patients how to deal with pain through biofeedback. At other times it is used simply to promote general good health.

Biofeedback works by providing tangible feedback on how the body reacts to stressful situations. During a typical session, electrical sensors are attached to the body as
15 a measuring device. These sensors can record the body's various reactions to stress, such as sweat or muscle contractions. The therapist then uses an indicator, perhaps a light or a sound, to create a visual or aural association for the patient. Every time the body reacts in a certain way, the indicator goes off. The patient is then instructed to try to control the sound or light, and in doing so learns to control his or her body.

20 Different forms of biofeedback therapy deal with different disorders. *Electromyograms, for example, measure muscle tension and can be helpful in treating backaches and headaches. Patients with circulatory problems and migraines benefit from temperature biofeedback, which records the temperature of the skin. *Galvanic skin response training measures perspiration, and is helpful in dealing with anxiety-related
25 disorders. And brainwaves can be charted and then used to treat insomnia; they also have the potential to be applied to a variety of neurological disorders.

Biofeedback seems effective in reducing patients' dependency on medicine and raising their awareness of how their bodies work. It also has the potential to significantly reduce medical costs. But the true medical value of biofeedback is still in question. Until
30 scientists can accurately explain how the therapy works and the exact means by which patients can control their bodily responses, a shadow of doubt will remain.

*electromyogram: a graphic record of the electric activity of muscle contractions
*galvanic skin response: a change in the skin caused by an emotional reaction to a stimulus

---

WORD
CHECK

Choose the correct words for the blanks from the highlighted words in the passage.

1. to cause sickness or problems: _____
2. related to the sense of hearing: _____
3. moisture lost through the skin: _____
4. a tightening of a muscle: _____

1 What is the best title for the passage?
  a. Biofeedback: A Cure-all Therapy for Patients
  b. Biofeedback: Having the Power to Heal Yourself
  c. Biofeedback: Effective When Used with Medicine
  d. Biofeedback: Interactive Functions between Body and Brain

2 Biofeedback makes it possible for patients to cure their disorders by _____.
  a. learning how their brain works
  b. controlling their bodily responses
  c. changing involuntary mental activities
  d. encountering different stressful situations

3 Which is closest in meaning to tangible?
  a. positive   b. valuable   c. perceptible   d. immediate

4 Put the following steps of biofeedback in order.
  a. recording reactions to stress
  b. attaching sensors to the body
  c. instructing a patient to control his or her reactions
  d. creating an association with stress through an indicator

5 Which is NOT mentioned as an advantage of biofeedback?
  a. It lowers dependency on medicine.
  b. It raises awareness of how the body functions.
  c. It substantially reduces medical costs.
  d. It cures serious illnesses without resorting to operations.

SUMMARY

6 Fill in the blanks to complete the topic of each paragraph.
  a. Paragraph 1: a form of therapy that helps humans _____
  b. Paragraph 2: _____ of biofeedback therapy
  c. Paragraph 3: _____
  d. Paragraph 4: _____ of biofeedback therapy
  e. Paragraph 5: the real and potential benefits of biofeedback

In linguistics, the type of speech a person uses is referred to as a code. A code can be a language, a dialect, or even an intonation or style. Code-switching occurs when a person changes his or her code during a conversation. Sometimes there is a very practical reason for this change. If a person is unable to express a thought in one code, he or she will switch to another.

Other times, however, the motivations behind code-switching can have more complex social implications. It can be a way of identifying a reassuring similarity with someone from the same geographic or socioeconomic background, such as with people who have immigrated to a new country. During the day, they'll speak their adopted language, but at home they mix it together with their native tongue. Code-switching can also be used to express perceived intellectual superiority. For instance, educated English speakers may add Latin or French phrases to flaunt their language skills.

Depending on the motivation behind the change, code-switching can be categorized as one of two types. Situational code-switching, as the name implies, occurs because of a change in situation. For example, a child at school might speak a dialect of urban slang in the playground but switch to standard English when entering the classroom. The motivation behind metaphorical code-switching, on the other hand, is a change in the topic of conversation. In Norway, official business is usually conducted in the Bokmal dialect. But when the topic changes to more casual subjects, the speakers will switch to the Nynorsk dialect.

Another qualification of code-switching is whether it is internal or external. Internal codeswitching occurs within a single language, with a change in tone or dialect. External codeswitching occurs between two different languages. In multilingual countries, such as India, external code-switching often happens in everyday conversation without even being noticed. Both internal and external code-switching can occur with either situational or metaphorical code-switching and vice versa.

Not everyone is bilingual, but most people have the ability to use more than one code. The ability to know when to switch from one to another is an integral part of the set of conversational skills that humans rely on to effectively express their feelings.

WORD CHECK

Choose the correct words for the blanks from the highlighted words in the passage.

1. pertaining to a certain area or region: _____
2. giving confidence and easing anxiety: _____
3. necessary to the completeness of the whole: _____
4. the act of being or appearing to be better than others: _____

1 **What is the best title for the passage?**
    a. When and Why Do You Switch Codes?
    b. What Is the Best Way to Learn Language Codes?
    c. Why Is Code-switching Important to Multilinguals?
    d. How Do Native Tongues Affect Second Language Learning?

2 **Which is NOT mentioned as a reason for code-switching?**
    a. to express ideas in an efficient manner
    b. to identify with people from the same group
    c. to demonstrate intellectual superiority
    d. to give a speaker's opinions confidently

3 **Which is closest in meaning to flaunt?**
    a. maintain   b. show off   c. practice   d. make use of

4 **What is the difference between internal and external code-switching?**
    _____

5 **Choose which terms apply in the situations below.**
    a. A boy doesn't use the same words or phrases when speaking to his grandfather as he does when speaking to his friends.
    (situational code-switching / metaphorical code-switching)
    b. In the U.S., Spanish speakers often combine Spanish and English words in the same sentence. This phenomenon has become so common that it is known as "Spanglish."
    (internal code-switching / external code-switching)

SUMMARY

6 **Summarize the topic of each paragraph.**
    a. Paragraph 1: _____
    b. Paragraph 2: _____
    c. Paragraph 3: _____
    d. Paragraph 4: _____
    e. Paragraph 5: _____

Globish

Globalization brings people of different cultures into contact with each other, often highlighting language barriers. Some believe that the best way to deal with language barriers is to create a completely artificial language for all the world's inhabitants to learn. Others, however, insist that this is impractical, proposing instead the simplification or alteration of a
5 language that is already in widespread use. The creation of Globish, a condensed version of English, was inspired by this idea.

Former vice president of IBM Jean-Paul Nerriere invented Globish after observing an interesting phenomenon in his professional travels. As a non-native English speaker, he experienced more success in communicating with other non-native speakers than his
10 native-speaking associates did. He concluded that non-native speakers do not actually speak standard English, but rather a simplified version of it. Combining the words "global" and "English," Nerriere termed this language system Globish; he then created an official list of its vocabulary and began promoting it as a tool for increasing the efficiency of international communication.

15 Central to Nerriere's creation are its differences from such wholly artificial languages as Esperanto and Interlingua. Because it is based on the English language, Globish builds on linguistic knowledge that people already possess instead of requiring them to learn a completely new language. In fact, Nerriere maintains that Globish is not a separate language at all since it does not represent a unique culture or history. Its aim is simply to take the
20 basic and most essential elements of English and disregard its more complex aspects. Speakers of Globish can communicate using only 1,500 words. For example, instead of learning the word "nephew," a speaker relies on the simpler phrase "the son of my brother" to communicate the same idea. Also, Globish employs only the most elementary of English's grammatical structures, and it holds that our assessment of pronunciation should
25 be based on intelligibility, not perfection.

Not all linguistic experts agree on the usefulness of Globish, however. ■ One of the most frequent criticisms is with the selection of Globish's vocabulary. ■ Furthermore, Nerriere's book explaining the pronunciation and grammar of Globish contains various inconsistencies, causing confusion among learners of the system. ■ Considering these
30 issues, Globish will probably require further development before it can be accepted on a larger scale. ■

---

1 The word this in the passage refers to

ⓐ highlighting language barriers

ⓑ creating a completely artificial language

ⓒ the simplification or alteration of a language

ⓓ the creation of Globish

2 According to paragraph 2, Nerriere got the idea for Globish from his conversations with

(a) speakers of Globish

(b) language experts

(c) native English speakers

(d) non-native English speakers

3 The word disregard in the passage is closest in meaning to

(a) consider   (b) ignore   (c) examine   (d) master

4 Which can be inferred about Globish from paragraph 3?

(a) It was inspired by the creation of Esperanto.

(b) It is spoken by more people than Interlingua is.

(c) It represents a unique cultural element of the U.S.

(d) It doesn't emphasize accurate pronunciation.

5 Look at the four squares [■] that indicate where the following sentence could be added to the passage.

It is not clear how the 1,500 words were chosen, and certain additions and omissions are seen as arbitrary.

Where would the sentence best fit?

6 Directions   An introductory sentence for a brief summary of the passage is provided below. Complete the summary by selecting the THREE answer choices that express the most important ideas in the passage.

Globish, a simplified version of English, is one example of an attempt to bridge the language barriers in today's world.

(a) Globish was created by Jean-Paul Nerriere and inspired by his experiences in international settings.

(b) Jean-Paul Nerriere coined the term Globish by mixing the words "global" and "English."

(c) With a vocabulary of only 1,500 words, Globish is difficult to communicate with.

(d) Globish is comprised of easy vocabulary, basic grammar and easy-to-understand pronunciation.

(e) Some people have found flaws with the way Globish was created and explained.

(f) Globish will most likely become a major international language.

Environmentalism has become a hot topic in recent years. We are starting to take a long look at the way we do things and then trying to find ecofriendly alternatives. When we think about
5 protecting the planet, however, we don't usually think too much about the clothes we wear. But consider this: Clothing manufacturers have been rapidly producing cheap garments in an effort to keep up with ever-changing fashion trends. The clothes may look good, but they are not made to last. They call it "fast
10 fashion," and it's taking a toll on the environment.

The textiles that companies elect to make their clothing from, cheap, nonbiodegradable synthetic materials such as nylon and polyester, are a big part of the problem. These fabrics are created through a manufacturing process that pollutes the atmosphere, and when they are thrown away they can end up in landfills that pollute
15 our ground water for years and years. Not only synthetic textiles but also the natural materials used in fast fashion, such as cotton, can damage the environment. There are more pesticides used in the commercial farming of cotton than with most other crops, and many of these textiles are later bleached or colored with artificial dyes, which adds to the ever-growing number of chemicals poisoning our world.

20 Eco fashion was born as an environmentally friendly response to these unsound practices. Instead of manufacturing clothes from harmful materials, eco fashion makes use of ecofriendly fibers, such as hemp, linen, and cotton that is grown organically. By coloring these fabrics with natural dyes made from plants and roots, companies can drastically reduce the amount of chemicals that goes into making each garment. Eco
25 fashion also utilizes old or discarded clothing and other recyclable materials to make new clothes and accessories, creating fashionable garments from items as diverse and unlikely as plastic bottles and bicycle tires. By recycling existing materials, the amount of waste that ends up in landfills is minimized and energy expenditure is reduced by cutting back on the amount of textiles shipped from abroad.

30 Although the eco fashion industry is still in its infancy, it represents a growing understanding of the importance of the decisions we make as consumers. What we choose to buy really can make a difference.

WORD CHECK

Choose the correct words for the blanks from the highlighted words in the passage.

1. to throw away: _____
2. an item of clothing: _____
3. made artificially or not of natural origin: _____
4. an early stage of development or growth: _____

1 What is the main idea of the passage?
   a. Eco fashion encourages fashion companies to be more profitable.
   b. Environmentally friendly fashion produces clothes of better quality.
   c. Fast fashion reflects a change in the unpredictable tastes of consumers.
   d. Efforts to preserve the environment are being made in the fashion industry.

2 What does the underlined part in paragraph 1 mean?
   a. It benefits the environment.
   b. It has a negative effect on the environment.
   c. It is under the influence of the environment.
   d. It collects funds to keep the environment clean.

3 According to the passage, cotton can be a threat to the environment because
   _____.
   a. it is a nonbiodegradable substance
   b. garments made from it are difficult to recycle
   c. it produces a large amount of waste when it is processed
   d. pesticides and chemicals are used in growing and processing it

4 Which is NOT included in the practice of eco fashion according to the passage?
   a. developing high-tech fabrics
   b. using organically grown cotton
   c. coloring fabrics with natural dyes
   d. making new fashion items using recyclable materials

5 What are the two benefits of recycling existing materials?
   _____

SUMMARY

6 Use the words in the box to fill in the blanks.

| recycles | benefits | eco fashion | damage | pesticides | synthetic | produces |

Clothing manufacturers are causing a lot of _____ to the environment through their focus on "fast fashion." Because these companies use nonbiodegradable _____ materials and chemical dyes, the manufacturing process poisons the environment. Even natural materials can damage the environment through the use of _____ and artificial dyes. In response to these unsound practices, _____ was started. It uses environmentally friendly materials and _____ old materials. This helps reduce waste and can really make a difference.

Technological advances over the past century have allowed human civilization to flourish. We live at a level of comfort and convenience that previous generations could scarcely have imagined. Unfortunately,
5 some of these advances have come at a troubling cost – endocrine disruptors.

The hormones our bodies produce are essential to our well-being since they play a role in a wide variety of vital life processes, including growth and reproduction. Endocrine disruptors are synthetic chemicals that <u>adversely</u> affect the production, distribution, and
10 behavior of these hormones, a disruption that can have catastrophic effects. Animals have long suffered from exposure to these contaminants, and there is reason to believe that humans are being directly affected as well.

Endocrine disruptors are found in a variety of man-made materials. When such materials are dumped into the environment, these harmful chemicals accumulate in the
15 fat of fish and animals that live nearby. If people eat these contaminated fish or animals, the endocrine disruptors can enter their systems. These chemicals can also become airborne during the manufacture or disposal of products that contain them, leading to the possibility of contamination through inhalation. They can also be absorbed through the skin by direct contact with pesticides, detergents, and other substances.

20 So _____(A)_____? Scientists have observed severe consequences in a variety of animal species, from alligators to eagles, including birth defects, malformed reproductive systems, and immune problems. Endocrine disruptors affect growth and development, and because of this there is a fear that unborn children are at the greatest risk. There is also evidence tying endocrine disruptors to an increase in the incidence of
25 reproductive cancer in young men.

The risk of exposure to endocrine disruptors can be reduced by eating organic food and avoiding the use of pesticides in your home. Fatty foods, such as cheese and meat, are best eaten in moderation and should not be stored in plastic containers or plastic wrap. No foods should be heated in any form of plastic. These steps may help you
30 avoid contamination, but they won't solve the problem faced by our society. Science and technology must come up with an effective way to clean up the mess they have made.

WORD
CHECK

Choose the correct words for the blanks from the highlighted words in the passage.

1. the rate of occurrence: _____
2. a thing that makes sth dirty: _____
3. with control or not in excess: _____
4. extremely damaging or harmful: _____

1 What is the best title for the passage?
   a. The Future of a Contaminated World
   b. The Threat of Endocrine Disruptors
   c. An Effective Way to Save Our Polluted World
   d. Finding a Way to Eliminate the Deadly Chemicals

2 Why are hormones essential to our well-being?

_____

3 Which is closest in meaning to adversely?
   a. uselessly   b. negatively   c. partially   d. regularly

4 Which is NOT mentioned as a route of exposure to endocrine disruptors?
   a. ingesting contaminated animals
   b. inhaling poisonous chemicals
   c. inheriting them from parents
   d. contacting unsafe substances directly

5 What is the best expression for blank (A)?
   a. how can we deal with endocrine disruptors
   b. how can we reveal the risk of endocrine disruptors
   c. what happens to living organisms which have been exposed
   d. what factors are associated with producing endocrine disruptors

SUMMARY

6 Match each main point to the correct paragraph in the passage.
   a. Paragraph 1 •   • ① Endocrine disruptors adversely affect our hormones.
   b. Paragraph 2 •   • ② Endocrine disruptors can enter animals and humans in a variety of ways.
   c. Paragraph 3 •   • ③ Some technological advances have caused problems.
   d. Paragraph 4 •   • ④ There are several ways of avoiding endocrine disruptors.
   e. Paragraph 5 •   • ⑤ Endocrine disruptors harm animals and possibly humans as well.

In Peru, approximately 50 km northwest of the former Incan capital city of Cuzco and about 3,500 meters above sea level, there is a stunning and mysterious series of Inca ruins. Called Moray, this archaeological site is composed of several enormous, bowl-like depressions, each formed by a series of circular terraces. Although the purpose that these depressions served is uncertain, most archaeologists agree that they were used to carry out agricultural research.

Moray has several amazing characteristics that would make it an ideal place for conducting agricultural research. First, there is a remarkable difference in temperature, as much as 15 °C, from the tops of the depressions to their lowest points. The result is that, much like a modern-day greenhouse, each depression contains several microclimate zones, small areas with their own unique climates. Even more incredibly, these different temperatures correspond to the natural climates of surrounding areas, from coastal farmland to high-elevation terraces. This would have allowed the Inca to study how different climatic conditions affected crops all in one place. Pollen studies have even shown that soils from different regions of the Inca Empire were imported to Moray. This would have made it possible to recreate the growing conditions in these different regions almost exactly.

The second remarkable feature of Moray is its drainage system. ⓐ Because of the depressions' bowl-shaped design, it seems like the lower parts of the depressions would easily fill up with water during heavy rain. ⓑ How the depressions drain remains a mystery, but it has been suggested that underground channels at the bottom may carry the water away. ⓒ Another theory suggests that the depressions are located over a natural rock formation that is highly porous, which would enable water to steadily filter out. ⓓ

Amazingly, about 60 percent of the world's food crops, including hundreds of varieties of maize and thousands of varieties of potato, originated in the Andes Mountains. This shows how good the indigenous population was at developing crops that were well suited to the region's different climates. Although we may never know conclusively why Moray was constructed, it is highly likely that the site was used to learn how to make the best use of the Inca Empire's diverse lands.

WORD
CHECK

Choose the correct words for the blanks from the highlighted words in the passage.

1. coming from a particular region: _____
2. an area that is lower than other areas near it: _____
3. an area of flat farmland built into a hillside: _____
4. a weather environment unique to a small region: _____

1 What is the best title for the passage?

   a. The Secrets of Agricultural Technology in Peru

   b. The Remarkable Drainage System of the Moray Ruins

   c. The Amazing Mysteries of the Moray Ruins

   d. The Complex Lives of the Incas in Peru

2 Why does the author mention a modern-day greenhouse in the paragraph 2?

   a. to compare its temperature range to that of the depressions

   b. to explain that its principle originated from the depressions

   c. to show an example of a place where diverse crops can grow well

   d. to say that it is one of the most mysterious things in modern times

3 Where would the following sentence best fit in paragraph 3?

> Even in heavy downpours, though, the structures never flood.

4 Which is NOT mentioned as evidence that Moray may have been a place for agricultural research?

   a. the temperature difference from the depressions' top to bottom

   b. the soil that was imported from different regions

   c. the irrigation channels in the lower parts of the depressions

   d. the drainage system that prevents water from filling up the depressions

5 According to paragraph 4, what shows how good the population of Moray was at developing crops?

_____

SUMMARY

6 Use the words in the box to fill in the blanks.

terraces	research	temperature	flood	construct	crop	filter

Moray

- Location: 50 km northwest of Cuzco, Peru
- Appearance: several bowl-shaped depressions with circular _____
- Likely purpose: agricultural _____ site
- Features:
  1. Microclimates
     - Different temperatures correspond to surrounding areas.
     - Soils from different parts of Inca Empire were used.
  2. Drainage system
     - Depressions never _____
     - Theories: Water goes through underground pathways.
       Porous rock lets water _____ out.

Decoding Egyptian Hieroglyphs

In 1799, French troops reconstructing a fort near an Egyptian town once known as Rosetta discovered an interesting object. Named the "Rosetta Stone," it turned out to be the key to deciphering ancient Egyptian *hieroglyphic script.

■ The Rosetta Stone was created in 196 B.C., the first anniversary of the coronation
5 of Ptolemy V Epiphanes, ruler of Egypt. ■ Its inscriptions declare Egyptian priests' support of Ptolemy and list the ways the country had benefited under his rule. ■ Scholars believe the stone was one of many such official acts designed to increase loyalty to Ptolemy among all Egyptians. ■

A smooth, dark gray slab that is about 112 centimeters tall and 75 centimeters wide,
10 the Rosetta Stone bears inscriptions of the exact same text in three different writing styles. First is Egyptian hieroglyphics, an ancient script used primarily for important religious documents of the time. Second is Demotic, a cursive-like script utilized by commoners during Ptolemy's reign. The final script is Greek, as the administrative heads of Egypt in this era, and indeed Ptolemy himself, were of Greek origin.

15 The Rosetta Stone's importance to *Egyptology is immense. Almost all ancient Egyptian texts were written in hieroglyphics, yet knowledge of this writing system had disappeared around A.D. 400 when it ceased to be used. For this reason, Egyptologists before 1800 had no way of accessing the information contained in such texts. The significance of the Rosetta Stone was that it provided a point of comparison between
20 hieroglyphic writing and the Greek language, allowing scholars to use the Greek inscription as a key to the translation of the hieroglyphs.

In the course of studying the stone, French Egyptologist Jean-François Champollion made a momentous discovery. Previously, it had been assumed that the hieroglyphic script was only intended to be read, not spoken. In other words, Egyptologists did not
25 think the hieroglyphs corresponded to specific spoken sounds. Champollion's conclusion to the contrary proved to be an enormous breakthrough, allowing researchers to translate countless hieroglyphic texts and gain invaluable information about ancient Egyptian civilization. Because of his work and that of many others, this chance discovery by French troops in 1799 is responsible for much of what we now know about ancient Egypt.

*hieroglyphic: related to a system of picture symbols employed in ancient Egypt
*Egyptology: the study of ancient Egyptian civilization

---

1 The word deciphering in the passage is closest in meaning to

ⓐ creating   ⓑ converting   ⓒ translating   ⓓ writing

2 Look at the four squares [■] that indicate where the following sentence could be added to the passage.

They also mention various honors and privileges granted to the ruler by the priests.

Where would the sentence best fit?

3 Which was true about Egypt during Ptolemy's time according to paragraph 3?

ⓐ Demotic script was looked down upon by religious officials.

ⓑ Most people in the country used hieroglyphic script.

ⓒ The administrative heads of state used a different script from the ordinary people.

ⓓ Most Egyptians were able to speak three different languages.

4 Which of the sentences below best expresses the essential information in the highlighted sentence in the passage?

ⓐ Scholars were able to use Greek to decode the Rosetta Stone's hieroglyphs.

ⓑ The inscriptions on the Rosetta Stone gave clues to the meaning of Greek.

ⓒ The Greek inscribed on the Rosetta Stone is more important than the hieroglyphs.

ⓓ The hieroglyphs on the Rosetta Stone provided an easy way for scholars to translate the Greek.

5 Why does the author mention Jean-François Champollion in paragraph 5?

ⓐ to refer the first person who learned to speak ancient Egyptian

ⓑ to suggest that most Egyptologists already understood hieroglyphic writing

ⓒ to explain an important achievement in the study of the Rosetta Stone

ⓓ to identify the leader of the French troops who found the Rosetta Stone

6 Directions An introductory sentence for a brief summary of the passage is provided below. Complete the summary by selecting the THREE answer choices that express the most important ideas in the passage.

An accidental discovery by French soldiers in Egypt in 1799 led to amazing advances in the understanding of the region's ancient civilization.

ⓐ Ptolemy V Epiphanes was the ruler of Egypt when the Rosetta Stone was created.

ⓑ The Rosetta Stone bears the same text in hieroglyphs, Demotic, and Greek.

ⓒ Demotic was the most widely used script in ancient Egypt.

ⓓ The hieroglyphic script disappeared from use in Egypt around A.D. 400.

ⓔ Its use as a tool of translation made the Rosetta Stone crucial to Egyptology.

ⓕ The finding that hieroglyphs could be spoken aloud enabled a new understanding of the script.

WORD REVIEW TEST

[1~3] Choose the word that is closest in meaning to the underlined one.

1. He's always <u>flaunting</u> how much money he has.
   a. turning out   b. going off   c. showing off   d. ending up

2. Hundreds of people lost their lives in a <u>catastrophic</u> earthquake.
   a. immense   b. disastrous   c. robust   d. temporary

3. She <u>accumulated</u> wealth through dishonest means.
   a. exchanged   b. planned   c. operated   d. gathered

[4~7] Connect each phrase in column B with its matching verb in column A.

A	B
4. clean up •	• a. fashion trends
5. decipher •	• b. an effective way
6. keep up with •	• c. the mess
7. come up with •	• d. the ancient script

[8~12] Choose the best word to complete each sentence. (Change the form if needed.)

conduct	ail	depression	discard	condense	privilege	perspiration

8. You need to _____ the food waste separately from other trash.

9. Her life's work is _____ in this book.

10. Excess bodily fluids are eliminated through _____.

11. If you become a member, you get a variety of _____.

12. _____ a scientific experiment involves a number of separate stages.

[13~16] Choose the correct word for each definition.

landfill	stunning	manner	expenditure	inconsistency	superiority	typical

13. an amount spent or used:

14. the act of being or appearing to be better than others:

15. extremely beautiful or impressive:

16. the quality of failing to agree or follow a pattern:

[17~22] Choose the best word to complete each sentence.

17. Information security is _____ to IT operations.
    a. alternative   b. synthetic   c. integral   d. extravagant

18. The security camera's pictures allowed the police to _____ the suspects.
    a. track down   b. resort to   c. leave out   d. look down upon

19. I _____ a traffic signal and was pulled over by a police officer.
    a. advocated   b. processed   c. identified   d. disregarded

20. We need _____ evidence to prove his guilt.
    a. arbitrary   b. tangible   c. artificial   d. involuntary

21. Her handwriting is so bad that we can't _____ her note.
    a. decipher   b. formulate   c. resurrect   d. provision

22. I don't trust Susie because her words and actions don't always _____.
    a. emerge   b. correspond   c. disappear   d. contradict

[23~25] Circle the odd one out in each group.

23. huge   remarkable   immense   enormous
24. essential   momentous   crucial   indigenous
25. fabric   textile   cloth   garment

[26] Read and write the right number of the correct definition for each sentence.

> **flourish** *v.* **1.** to be in a vigorous state or to be successful: *Buddhism flourished during Goryeo Dynasty.* **2.** to grow well or luxuriantly: *to flourish in the rich soil* **3.** to wave sth in your hand in order to make people notice it: *He flourished the handkerchief to emphasize the point.*

    a. She flourished her hat to the crowd. _____
    b. Grass doesn't flourish in dry climates. _____

Y ou've seen them come to life on the movie screen. They're not really alive, but their movements seem real and their faces show emotion. So what makes the characters in movies like *Polar Express* and *Avatar* seem so lifelike? It's the fact that they 5 were all created with a combination of acting and digital effects called "performance capture."

Performance capture is a refinement of a special effects technique called motion capture. Motion capture is what makes artificial figures move so realistically in animation movies and 10 video games. It's created by capturing the motions of an actual person and applying them to a computer-generated character. But performance capture takes this one step further, recording not only general body movements but also subtle facial expressions.

To bring a character to life through performance capture, an actor's face and body are first covered in small sensors. The actor then enters a special black box and performs 15 while infrared cameras record the action from four angles, creating a three-dimensional effect. Using these recordings, software digitally transfers the actor's performance onto computer-generated characters. The characters are then projected onto a highly detailed virtual set, complete with virtual props and virtual costumes, and the illusion of reality is complete.

20 For a filmmaker, performance capture offers a faster alternative to traditional time-consuming animation methods; it also creates movements and facial expressions that are more natural. And, compared to scenes using live actors, there is more control over the editing process. If something goes wrong with the shot, it doesn't need to be re-filmed. It can just be retouched on the computer. And from an actor's point of view, 25 performance capture is advantageous because it lets him or her act using complex facial expressions that in the past would have been lost beneath latex masks or special effects. It can even allow a single actor to play multiple roles, such as in *Polar Express*, where Tom Hanks portrayed five different characters, including Santa Claus and a young boy.

Performance capture brings filmmakers the best of both worlds, affording a workable 30 balance between the skills of actors and the abilities of special effects technicians. As a result, millions of viewers are rewarded with dazzling scenes of movie magic.

WORD CHECK

Choose the correct words for the blanks from the highlighted words in the passage.

1. a change that improves sth: _____
2. fine or delicate in meaning or intent: _____
3. to cause sth to appear on a distant surface: _____
4. to play a certain role in a TV show, play or movie: _____

1 What is the best title for the passage?

  a. Motion Capture vs. Performance Capture
  b. A More Convenient Digital Film Editing Method
  c. A Digital Technique that Brings Characters to Life
  d. Amazing Virtual Characters in Breathtaking Movies

2 Why is performance capture a more refined special effects technique than motion capture?

  _____

3 Put the following steps of performance capture in order.

  a. having an actor perform inside a special black box
  b. attaching small sensors to an actor's face and body
  c. adding digital characters to a virtual set
  d. transferring an actor's performance onto digital characters

4 Which is NOT mentioned as a merit of performance capture?

  a. It saves a lot of time when making a movie with virtual characters.
  b. It helps editors to match sound to visual images.
  c. It enables actors to demonstrate subtle facial expressions.
  d. It makes it possible for an actor to play several characters in a movie.

5 Which CANNOT be inferred about performance capture from the passage?

  a. It is commonly used for virtual character creation.
  b. It is a more developed technique than motion capture.
  c. It is carried out using computer techniques.
  d. It guarantees filmmakers box-office success.

SUMMARY

6 Match each topic to the correct paragraph in the passage.

  a. Paragraph 1 •   • ① the steps used in performance capture
  b. Paragraph 2 •   • ② the technique used to give life to animated characters
  c. Paragraph 3 •   • ③ the influence of performance capture on filmmakers
                               and viewers
  d. Paragraph 4 •   • ④ the advantages of performance capture
  e. Paragraph 5 •   • ⑤ the difference between motion and performance
                               capture

The famous actor Marlon Brando is known for his powerhouse performances in some of Hollywood's biggest blockbusters. Marilyn Monroe and James Dean are both movie legends, admired even after death for the film personas they
5　created. And all three of them cast their on-screen spells using a technique known as "method acting."

Method actors seek to create realistic performances by analyzing and understanding the psychological motivations behind the actions of the characters they portray. The technique
10　was initially developed by Konstantin Stanislavski in Russia around the turn of the 20th century. And it enjoyed a resurgence in the United States in the 1950s when it was popularized by Lee Strasberg, an American director, producer, and acting teacher.

Method acting places great demands upon the actors who use it, requiring them to create complex emotions for people that don't exist outside of a script. They construct
15　entire histories for the characters they are playing, using imaginary experiences and events in order to better understand why the characters act and feel the way they do. The actors then attempt to recreate these feelings within themselves, delving into their personal memories for experiences that generate similar emotions. If method acting is done correctly, the actors become completely immersed, and it can result in frighteningly
20　realistic performances, the kind that movie-goers don't easily forget.

But method acting requires a great deal of discipline and can take a severe mental and physical toll on performers. Some actors immerse themselves so deeply that they place themselves _____(A)_____. This has manifested itself in such things as experimental drug use, which in the case of River Phoenix actually led to death from a drug overdose.
25　A more common and less serious negative result is simply _____(B)_____. Poorly executed method acting has resulted in some of the least impressive performances in movie history.

But along with unskilled performers who are unable to pull off the demanding requirements of method acting, there have been some modern Hollywood stars who have successfully applied it to their roles, including Al Pacino, Robert De Niro, and Dustin
30　Hoffman. The power of their performances proves that there is potential for exceptional results from this unique approach to acting.

WORD CHECK

Choose the correct words for the blanks from the highlighted words in the passage.

1. to involve deeply or absorb: _____
2. to show plainly or demonstrate: _____
3. to accomplish or achieve sth difficult: _____
4. a personality that is displayed but may not be real: _____

1 **What is the best title for the passage?**
   a. The Bible for Hollywood Movie Stars
   b. A Standard Way of Creating Characters
   c. Potential Disadvantages of Method Acting
   d. A Demanding but Rewarding Acting Technique

2 **What does the underlined part in paragraph 1 imply?**
   a. They made a fortune from appearing in popular movies.
   b. They were awarded prizes for their film roles.
   c. Audiences were fascinated by their performances.
   d. The movies they starred in enjoyed good reputations.

3 **Method actors approach their performances by _____.**
   a. experiencing physical pain
   b. bringing out their hidden talents
   c. psychologically immersing themselves in the characters' roles
   d. analyzing and understanding other successful actors' performances

4 **What is the best pair for blanks (A) and (B)?**

(A)	(B)
a. in danger	— bad acting
b. into a confused state	— severe criticism
c. in a competitive position	— violent performances
d. at the center of criticism	— losing their reputation

5 **Which is NOT true about method acting according to the passage?**
   a. It emphasizes a psychological approach to acting.
   b. It was first developed in Russia and later became popular in the United States.
   c. Actors need lots of training to base performances on it.
   d. Famous actors starring in blockbusters commonly use it.

SUMMARY

6 Use the words in the box to fill in the blanks.

| technique   motivations   resurgence   hide   performances   problems   recreate |

Method acting is a _____ that has resulted in some of the greatest _____ in movie history. It focuses on the deep inner _____ of characters to provide realistic acting. Method actors try to understand the emotions of their characters and _____ them in themselves. This can lead to _____ for actors, as well as bad portrayals. Nevertheless, when done well, method acting can result in memorable performances from actors.

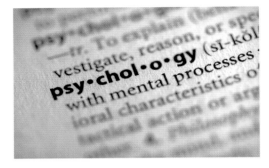

Describing Sigmund Freud's ideas about the mind, someone once said that the human personality is "basically a battlefield ... a dark cellar in which a well-bred spinster and a
5 pleasure-seeking monkey are forever engaged in mortal combat, the struggle being refereed by a rather nervous bank clerk." To understand what these odd characters have to do with personality, one must analyze the makeup of the mind as Freud imagined it.

10 Think of the mind as an iceberg. The visible tip of the iceberg is comparable to our conscious, the small portion of the mind that we are aware of. The vast majority of the mind is our unconscious, lying below our awareness like the mass of an iceberg immersed in water. Freud's partitioning of the mind into these two sectors was later incorporated into a more comprehensive conception, the structural theory, which attempted to better
15 describe the mind's complexity by dividing it into three parts: the id, the superego, and the ego.

According to Freud's theory, the id is the part of the mind that is completely buried in the unconscious. The instinctive drives that motivate humans to pursue pleasure and avoid pain originate there. The next partition of the human mind is termed the superego.
20 Partly conscious, the superego acts as a moral conscience, regulating the desires of the id with its concepts of right and wrong. Finally, Freud's third division of the mind, the ego, operates mostly at the level of conscious thought. Concerned with external reality, the ego is aware of others' needs and perceives that the tendencies of the id and the superego need to be tempered.

25 It is obvious that the interplay of the three parts of the mind is quite essential, for they mesh together to form a personality that interacts smoothly with the world. With overpowering ids, people would only care about the fulfillment of their desires and have no concern for others. With dominating superegos, people would be extremely narrow-minded and would likely lead lonely lives due to their inability to accept moral
30 faults in others. And finally, the ego is indispensable to _____(A)_____, because without it people would be unable to harmonize the contrasting desires of the id and the superego.

Choose the correct words for the blanks from the highlighted words in the passage.

1. to make sth less extreme: _____
2. sth that tells right from wrong: _____
3. to include or use as part of sth: _____
4. to make sure others obey the rules of a contest or competition: _____

1 **What is the passage mainly about?**

    a. how to control the human unconscious

    b. Freud's categorization of the human mind

    c. crucial problems with Freud's theory of psychology

    d. the relationship between personality and intellectual ability

2 **Match each part of the mind with each character.**

    a. the id   •   • ① a well-bred spinster

    b. the superego •   • ② a pleasure-seeking monkey

    c. the ego   •   • ③ a rather nervous bank clerk

3 **Which of the following is NOT true according to the passage?**

    a. The mind is largely dominated by our unconscious.

    b. The id directs us to seek pleasure with regard to external reality.

    c. The superego is the moral part of the mind and develops ethical concepts.

    d. The ego juggles the demands of the id and superego.

4 **What is the best expression for blank (A)?**

    a. social success

    b. self-satisfaction

    c. a balanced personality

    d. intellectual development

5 **Which personality factor is dominant in the situation below?**

> As Betty approached a traffic light, it turned red. Since no other cars were in sight, she sped through the intersection.

    a. id   b. ego   c. superego   d. unconscious

SUMMARY

6 **Fill in the blank to complete the topic of each paragraph.**

    a. Paragraph 1: the three _____ living in the mind

    b. Paragraph 2: _____ to explain the mind

    c. Paragraph 3: _____

    d. Paragraph 4: _____ of the three divisions of the mind

Cognitive Dissonance

A person's worldview is made up of countless cognitions, pieces of information including facts, beliefs, values, and feelings. Throughout life, a person continually takes on new cognitions as new information is encountered. If, during the process, a new cognition conflicts with a previously held cognition, the result is called "cognitive dissonance."

5 Cognitive dissonance creates a sense of discomfort. For example, a man buys an expensive car because he thinks it gets good gas mileage. He then sees a commercial for a cheaper car that gets even better mileage. The man naturally feels upset because his initial cognition is in conflict with the new cognition.

People have a natural urge to avoid cognitive dissonance, and this can be done 10 in many ways. ■ The man in the previous example could simply choose to ignore the commercial. ■ Another method of eliminating the dissonance would be to introduce new cognitions to the situation. ■ The man could begin to emphasize other positive features of his car, thereby lessening the importance of gas mileage and price. ■ And, if the feeling of dissonance became extreme enough, the man might trade in his car for the second one.

15 It is easy to discount the power of cognitive dissonance, but it has been proven in various experiments. In the 1950s, researcher Leon Festinger studied the members of a cult who had been told by their leader that aliens would destroy Earth on a certain date. After the day came and nothing happened, cult members became even more loyal to their leader. Festinger explained that, instead of accepting the cognition that they had been fooled, 20 members chose to believe the leader's new message – the aliens had spared the planet to save the cult.

Obviously, cognitive dissonance can lead people to act in nonsensical ways. However, it also has the potential for positive uses, such as conflict resolution. Cognitive dissonance challenges previously held beliefs and values and can force people to revise them. In a war, 25 each side may view the other as inhuman or even evil. A tactic to counter this cognition might be to discuss or give examples of the enemy's family life and emphasize similarities between the two groups. By showing each side aspects of the other's humanity, the initial stereotype can be challenged and possibly overcome by the power of cognitive dissonance.

---

1 Which can be inferred about cognitions from paragraph 1?

ⓐ No one knows very much about them.

ⓑ Not all of them conflict with each other.

ⓒ Most of them are created during childhood.

ⓓ They only are formed when we are young.

2 In paragraph 2, what was the man's initial cognition?

    ⓐ his desire for a cheaper car

    ⓑ the commercial that he saw

    ⓒ his belief that he bought the right car

    ⓓ the fact that there was a better car available

3 Look at the four squares [■] that indicate where the following sentence could be added to the passage.

Then, in the future, he might attempt to avoid watching television commercials.

Where would the sentence best fit?

4 Why does the author mention the research of Leon Festinger in paragraph 4?

    ⓐ to suggest a useful application for cognitive dissonance

    ⓑ to discuss a theory that tried to disprove cognitive dissonance

    ⓒ to explain why the effects of cognitive dissonance are negative

    ⓓ to illustrate how the power of cognitive dissonance was demonstrated

5 The word counter in the passage is closest in meaning to

    ⓐ assist   ⓑ spread   ⓒ go against   ⓓ give up

6   Directions An introductory sentence for a brief summary of the passage is provided below. Complete the summary by selecting the THREE answer choices that express the most important ideas in the passage.

A person's point of view is composed of many cognitions that are constantly being added to.

    ⓐ When one cognition conflicts with another, it makes us feel uncomfortable.

    ⓑ Introducing new cognitions is one way that cognitive dissonance can be lessened.

    ⓒ The desire to eliminate feelings of dissonance can cause people to do irrational things.

    ⓓ Festinger's study shows the difficulty of accepting new cognitions.

    ⓔ Cognitive dissonance offers a possible solution to negative behaviors.

    ⓕ Cognitive dissonance could be used as a tool in conflict resolution, but this has so far been unsuccessful.

The word "twixter" was coined to refer to a new social group that exists somewhere between adolescence and adulthood, a group that is rapidly growing all around the world. It was derived from the word "betwixt," which has the same meaning as "between."

Twixters are "twentysomethings" who are no longer adolescents, but are not yet
5 behaving like typical adults. They're more concerned with enjoying their lives than saving up money, changing jobs often as they expect a lot more from a job than a paycheck. Many of them still live at home, relying on their parents for financial support. Without a proper income, twixters are reluctant to pursue two of the basic elements by which our society defines adulthood: marriage and a home.

10 No one cause can be singled out as being responsible for the twixter lifestyle. Instead, it appears to be a combination of various factors. Rising unemployment rates and slow economic growth have made it more difficult than ever to start a career. It has also been suggested that the college experience isn't properly preparing students for real-world jobs. Furthermore, the rising costs of higher education mean that many
15 twixters graduate under the burden of heavy debt, extending the time it takes to achieve financial independence.

As twixters continue to increase in numbers, they are beginning to reveal themselves as a serious burden on society. Some economists see them as a bleak omen of a future in which succeeding generations become caught in the same destructive economic cycle.
20 If twixters never fully accept their adulthood, the world may be faced with a generation devoid of economic and political leaders.

Views on twixters differ. Some sociologists and psychologists focus on the positive aspects. They feel the twixters are simply taking advantage of the benefits that an affluent society offers. They're extending the relatively carefree years of adolescence in order to
25 prepare for the rigors of adulthood, trying out different career paths and lifestyles before committing to one. But others see them in a more negative light, as _____(A)_____ who are not equipped with the necessary tools to survive on their own. So for some, twixters represent a _____(B)_____, while for
30 others they are nothing more than an unwanted social group of people who never outgrow their laziness.

WORD CHECK

Choose the correct words for the blanks from the highlighted words in the passage.

1. severity or hardship: _____

2. completely lacking or absent: _____

3. without hope or encouragement: _____

4. following in order of occurrence: _____

1   What is the best title for the passage?

a. Twixters – Leading a Stable Life
b. Twixters – Neither Adolescents nor Adults
c. Twixters – The Economic Engine of the Future
d. Twixters – The Jobless among the Highly Educated

2   According to the passage, all of the following describe features of twixters EXCE PT

a. making a fortune for the future
b. making frequent career changes
c. leaning on their parents financially
d. rejecting traditional adult roles

3   Which is NOT mentioned as being a cause of the twixter lifestyle?

a. an economic slowdown
b. a college experience inappropriate for preparing to find employment
c. a lack of a sense of belonging
d. the increasing costs of higher education

4   According to some economists, what may happen if twixters don't accept their adulthood?

_____

5   What is the best pair for blanks (A) and (B)?

	(A)		(B)
a.	failed adults	—	generation of idealists
b.	egoistic people	—	group of workaholics
c.	arrogant adults	—	generation of realists
d.	aimless people	—	group of humanists

SUMMARY

6   Use the words in the box to fill in the blanks.

adulthood   burden   economy   debt   education   advantage   carefree

Twixters are people in their 20s who are stuck between adolescence and _____.
They tend to stay unmarried, living with their parents and changing jobs often. This
phenomenon has many causes, including the high cost of _____ and rising
unemployment rates. There are worries that twixters will harm the _____ as
they grow older. While some people see them as _____ idealists, others view
twixters as lazy failures.

Terrorism seeks to bring about social or political changes through the generation of fear. This fear is usually used to weaken the power and influence of the status quo. Although the modern concept of terrorism has been around since the late 19th century, the sheer scale of the September 11th, 2001 terrorist attacks in the United States sent shock waves of fear across the entire world.

Terrorism has existed throughout history. Groups that have been alienated because of religious persecution, political oppression, economic exploitation, cultural domination, ethnic discrimination, or any combination of these usually perpetrate it. In some cases, extremists who believe that their faith is the one true religion have turned to terrorism. Sometimes, terrorist acts are committed by people who feel that their rights are being denied or that they have no legal outlets. Modern terrorism is often incited by the wide disparities in wealth we see throughout the world.

The September 11th terrorist attacks were extreme, but they serve as a prime example of the increasing deadliness of modern terrorism. Terrorism is not made up of _____(A)_____ acts of violence. Each attack is planned carefully as a means to a specific end. Targets are meticulously chosen, often selected to maximize fear by taking the lives of innocent civilians. These efforts are coordinated with great precision, all in the interest of creating fear and gaining media attention. And as terrorist groups seek international attention in today's globalized society, they've been progressively escalating their attacks in order to achieve this aim.

Although the most obvious effect of terrorism is the loss of human life, it also has the potential to strike an economic blow. Property damage and subsequent insurance claims after an attack often add up to enormous amounts. The financial world can be disrupted by fear, which sometimes even causes stock markets to crash. Because of this, terrorism has the potential to stunt economic growth, or perhaps even to collapse a national economy. And as terrorism steps up to a global scale, it is the global economy that is affected.

If modern terrorism is to be prevented, its causes must be understood. Whatever the underlying motivations of terrorist groups are, there is no excuse for vicious actions that affect innocent civilians.

WORD
CHECK

Choose the correct words for the blanks from the highlighted words in the passage.

1. to cause feelings of not belonging: _____
2. extremely carefully and precisely: _____
3. to commit a negative act: _____
4. to prevent sth from growing or developing as much as it should: _____

1 **What is the best title for the passage?**
    a. Terrorism for No Specific Reason
    b. The Modern Concept of Terrorism
    c. Global Cooperation to Prevent Modern Terrorism
    d. The Fear and Damage Resulting from Modern Terrorism

2 **Which is closest in meaning to incited?**
    a. provoked   b. originated
    c. changed   d. replaced

3 **What is the best expression for blank (A)?**
    a. random   b. cruel
    c. justified   d. unacceptable

4 **Which of the following is NOT true according to the passage?**
    a. Blind faith in a certain religion can sometimes cause terrorism.
    b. The unequal distribution of wealth can be one of the causes of terrorism.
    c. Terrorists try to avoid coverage by the media.
    d. Fear generated by terrorism can lead to the collapse of a national economy.

SUMMARY

5 **Fill in the blanks to complete the topic of each paragraph.**
    a. Paragraph 1: terrorism's goal of _____ around the world
    b. Paragraph 2: _____ that lead to terrorism
    c. Paragraph 3: how terrorism tries to _____
    d. Paragraph 4: the enormous _____ of terrorism
    e. Paragraph 5: completely rejecting terrorists' actions

It has long been recognized that both biological and environmental factors are involved in shaping personalities. Those traits that are genetically determined are referred to as an individual's "temperament."

5 Researchers have identified nine temperament traits that characterize young children during their early years of development. None of these traits are absolute; rather, every child exhibits each of these traits to a greater or lesser extent. Specifically, the behaviors relate to physical energy, the 10 regularity of biological functions, initial response to an unfamiliar environment or new people, adaptability to long-term change, the intensity of a child's reaction to a situation, a predisposition to being distracted by external events, persistence in task-solving, general sensitivity to the environment, and overall mood or demeanor.

Based upon which of these traits are manifest, a child's personality can be 15 categorized as belonging to one of three types. The "easy" child tends to adapt easily to new environments, has smooth biological functions, and is usually cheerful and in a good mood. The "difficult" child, on the other hand, has irregular biological functions, shows a negative response to new situations, and is slow to adapt to new environments or people. Somewhere in-between is the "slow-to-warm-up" child who has a slightly 20 negative response to new situations but can adapt more easily than the latter type. In addition, their bodily functions are not as regular as the "easy" child.

The inborn temperament of children _____(A)_____. An "easy" child will adapt more readily to family life and routines, thereby lessening the likelihood of adding additional stress to the family network. More intense children will likely generate 25 greater tension between themselves, parents, and siblings by upsetting family dynamics that may already be quite volatile, particularly if the other family members are also of a difficult nature.

Parents should analyze the temperament of their children, not simply as an academic exercise, but as a means for better understanding them both as individuals and members 30 of the family unit. By recognizing the inborn traits of their children, parents can respond to them in a positive way and try to influence their personal growth rather than simply compel them to change. This will help children learn how to deal with others in socially acceptable ways and lead to less friction within the home.

WORD CHECK

Choose the correct words for the blanks from the highlighted words in the passage.

1. the way sb behaves: _____
2. a state of conflict between people: _____
3. the quality of occurring in a predictable pattern: _____
4. a condition that makes sb behave in a particular way: _____

1 What is the passage mainly about?
   a. the process of analyzing the temperament of children
   b. children's differing behaviors toward new environments
   c. the importance of family during the early years of childhood
   d. the influence of children's temperament in shaping their personalities

2 What is the best expression for blank (A)?
   a. develops differently based on family types
   b. will obviously have an impact on family life
   c. can improve relationships between family members
   d. has nothing to do with the temperament of family members

3 Which is closest in meaning to volatile?
   a. timid   b. inactive   c. unstable   d. balanced

4 According to the passage, why should parents analyze the temperament of their children?

_____

5 Which CANNOT be inferred from the passage?
   a. A child's personality includes the three types equally.
   b. The "easy" child exhibits regular eating and sleeping patterns.
   c. The "difficult" child needs more time to get used to new people.
   d. The "slow-to-warm-up" child can adapt to new situations more easily than the "difficult" child.

SUMMARY

6 Fill in the blanks to complete the topic of each paragraph.
   a. Paragraph 1: _____
   b. Paragraph 2: _____
   c. Paragraph 3: _____
   d. Paragraph 4: _____
   e. Paragraph 5: how understanding children's temperament can help them develop

The Montessori Teaching Method

Dr. Maria Montessori (1870 –1952), the first woman in Italy to qualify as a physician, became interested in child development through her work on childhood diseases. Over time, she cultivated a particular interest in children deemed unable to be educated. From her observations of such children, she went on to create the Montessori method for the

5 education of low-income students. Montessori's notions were strongly influenced by the 18th century philosopher Jean-Jacques Rousseau, who set out his views on education in the classic work *Emile*. The Montessori method later became a well-known alternative to conventional educational techniques.

The goal of the Montessori teaching method is to provide students with a stimulating

10 environment. One of Dr. Montessori's learning principles was "first the education of the senses, then the education of the intellect." As such, Montessori classrooms reflect a truly "hands-on" approach to learning, as activities and learning objects are designed to engage all the senses during the learning process.

At the primary level, students are divided into two age groups: from birth to age six,

15 and from six through twelve. ■ The initial level is called the "children's house" and focuses on individual learning and self-paced development. ■ At the second level, students undergo "cosmic education," in which collaboration with others is encouraged as part of their development. ■ Rather than teacher-centered approaches that tend to dominate in the traditional school system, Montessori classrooms are student-centered, encouraging each

20 student to develop uniquely. ■

Every activity that students undertake is self-contained and leads to a new level of understanding upon completion. Although activities are sequenced, there is no prescribed timetable as to when tasks should be finished. A Montessori instructor, much like the teacher in *Emile*, observes rather than instructs students, providing them with appropriate

25 lessons at appropriate times.

There have been a number of criticisms brought against the Montessori method. Some believe that the sequenced learning activities stifle, rather than foster, a child's creativity. Others find fault with the fact that Montessori pupils are rarely assigned homework as it would be troublesome because of the teaching methodology and the

30 learning materials used in class. Yet despite its critics, Montessori schools continue to be popular with a certain segment of the population a half century after their founder's death.

---

1 The word conventional in the passage is closest in meaning to

   ⓐ simple   ⓑ mainstream   ⓒ efficient   ⓓ impractical

2 Which can be inferred about Montessori classrooms from paragraph 2?

  (a) Textbooks are not used by the students.

  (b) Multiple teachers share the task of educating students.

  (c) Students are allowed to choose which activities to undertake.

  (d) Students are more active than those in traditional classrooms.

3 Look at the four squares [■] that indicate where the following sentence could be added to the passage.

Montessori schools for students older than this are not as widespread, but they do exist.

Where would the sentence best fit?

4 Why does the author mention *Emile* in paragraph 4?

  (a) to identify the origin of sequenced learning tasks

  (b) to remind readers that Montessori was also an author

  (c) to show the inspiration behind the Montessori teacher's role

  (d) to give an example of a book all Montessori students must read

5 According to paragraph 5, why are some people critical of the Montessori method?

  (a) It is an out-of-date teaching method.

  (b) Its students spend too much time in class.

  (c) It restrains students' creativity.

  (d) It always allows students to get their own way.

6 `Directions` An introductory sentence for a brief summary of the passage is provided below. Complete the summary by selecting the THREE answer choices that express the most important ideas in the passage.

Dr. Maria Montessori created an innovative teaching method after studying the developmental processes of children with learning difficulties.

  (a) Although trained as a doctor, Montessori changed her focus to education.

  (b) Influenced by Rousseau, Montessori emphasized sensory stimulation in the classroom.

  (c) Students are grouped by age, but their tasks are based on individual needs.

  (d) Many Montessori schools are revising the sequences of their learning activities.

  (e) The lack of a timetable is considered a serious limitation of the method.

  (f) The Montessori method has its critics but continues to be widely practiced.

WORD REVIEW TEST

[1~4] Choose the word that is closest in meaning to the underlined one.

1. Warm clothing is <u>indispensable</u> in cold weather.
    a. desirable   b. essential   c. rewarding   d. inappropriate

2. The accounts were prepared <u>meticulously</u> by Mr. Davies.
    a. progressively   b. initially   c. carefully   d. frighteningly

3. Thanks to its strong teamwork, our team <u>pulled off</u> a win.
    a. accomplished   b. celebrated   c. escalated   d. immersed

4. If a pregnant woman drinks alcohol, it can <u>stunt</u> the growth of the fetus.
    a. stimulate   b. restrict   c. accelerate   d. transfer

[5~8] Connect each phrase in column B with its matching verb in column A.

A	B
5. portray •	• a. a word
6. coin •	• b. homework
7. assign •	• c. a character
8. strike •	• d. a blow

[9~12] Choose the best word to complete each sentence. (Change the form if needed.)

mesh   perpetrate   subsequent   omen   execute   affluent   awareness

9. The plan succeeded because it was well _____.

10. He left his artwork to be enjoyed by _____ generations.

11. Many people believe that a broken mirror is a bad _____.

12. A number of crimes were _____ by the criminals.

[13~16] Choose the correct word for each definition.

prop   dissonance   resurgence   coordinate   instinctive   persistence   cult

13. taking place without thought or planning: _____

14. an object used in a performance: _____

15. the ability to do sth in spite of difficulties: _____

16. a lack of unity or order: _____

[17~22] Choose the best word to complete each sentence.

17. I was unable to overcome my _____ to eat.
   a. trait   b. urge   c. combat   d. stereotype

18. His happiness was _____ in his smile.
   a. counter   b. manifest   c. regular   d. affordable

19. The diamond sparkled with _____ brilliance.
   a. volatile   b. irrational   c. cosmic   d. dazzling

20. Chameleons use their color-changing ability as a survival _____.
   a. tendency   b. tactic   c. friction   d. figure

21. There are _____ differences between American and Canadian English.
   a. virtual   b. mortal   c. subtle   d. nonsensical

22. The future seems _____ now that I have lost my job.
   a. bleak   b. random   c. carefree   d. sheer

[23~25] Circle the odd one out in each group.

23. segment   sector   partition   collaboration
24. persecution   exploitation   discrimination   predisposition
25. ignore   alienate   temper   discount

[26] Read and write the right number of the correct definition for each sentence.

> **project** *v.* **1.** to make plans for or plan ahead: *His new store is projected to open in July.*
> **2.** to predict or estimate based on data: *Recently she has been busy projecting next year's*
> *expenses.* **3.** to cause (an image) to appear on a surface: *to project the slides* **4.** to send
> out or cast into space: *to project a missile*

   a. The population in Seoul is projected to decrease. _____
   b. Many interesting pictures were projected onto the screen. _____

Its chemical name is $C_8H_7N_3O_2$. In its natural state, it is a yellowish crystal that is quite unremarkable. However, when mixed with an appropriate oxidant such as hydrogen peroxide, it becomes anything but ordinary. It can bring evidence to light at crime scenes that would otherwise be invisible to the naked eye.

5 Known as "luminol," this compound will glow a certain color when activated by a catalyst. Luminol takes on a bright blue-green glow in the presence of certain paints, chemical products, plants, and most importantly, iron. Since blood contains some iron, luminol allows investigators to detect blood, even when it has been cleaned away or has remained at the crime scene for years. When luminol is sprayed on a suspicious area in a 10 darkened room, it will glow blue-green if there are any traces of blood.

The chemistry behind this is rather straightforward. The iron acts to accelerate an oxidized chemical reaction between the hydrogen peroxide and luminol. During this reaction, the luminol loses hydrogen and nitrogen atoms while gaining oxygen atoms, resulting in a new chemical compound in a highly energized state. Most atoms that have 15 this boosted energy, however, return almost immediately back to their previous states, releasing excess energy along the way. Therefore, in the case of luminol, the electrons in the oxygen atoms return to a lower energy level and release their extra energy as a bluish green glow.

One would think that luminol would routinely be used during violent 20 crime investigations. However, the fact is that it is usually resorted to when other methods of investigation have been exhausted. The reason for this is that luminol breaks down genetic material that it comes into contact with. Its greatest asset — being able to detect even minute traces of blood — is, ironically, its greatest risk to investigators. Because these blood samples 25 are so small originally, spraying luminol on them can render them useless as *forensic evidence. Yet, when investigators are unable to find evidence of blood on their own, they hope that the luminol gamble will pay off by providing them with usable samples.

*forensic: related to the investigation and establishment of facts to be presented in court

WORD CHECK

Choose the correct words for the blanks from the highlighted words in the passage.

1. to succeed: _____
2. to cause to become: _____
3. to emit light without using fire: _____
4. to cause sth to happen faster: _____

1 What is the passage mainly about?

    a. luminol's colorful chemical reaction

    b. the danger of luminol as a compound

    c. the use of luminol to find traces of blood

    d. the most common method of detecting iron

2 Luminol is used during crime investigations because _____.

    a. it reacts with nothing but blood

    b. it can detect the iron that blood contains

    c. it can extract DNA and other genetic materials

    d. it gives off energy after coming into contact with blood

3 What role does iron play in the chemical reaction according to paragraph 3?

    _____

4 What does the underlined part in paragraph 4 mean?

    a. Luminol is a dangerously toxic chemical.

    b. The chances of detecting blood through luminol are low.

    c. Luminol can detect blood but may damage blood samples.

    d. It requires a special technique to analyze the results from a luminol reaction.

5 Which of the following is NOT true according to the passage?

    a. Luminol glows blue-green when it detects certain paints or blood.

    b. Luminol can detect blood that has remained hidden for several years.

    c. The reaction between the hydrogen peroxide and luminol creates excess energy.

    d. In violent crime investigations, luminol is usually used before any other method of investigation.

SUMMARY

6 Use the words in the box to fill in the blanks.

accelerate	glow	excess	asset	render	iron	destroy

Luminol is a chemical compound which will _____ a certain color when activated by a catalyst. Because of this characteristic, it can be used to detect evidence at crime scenes. When it's mixed with hydrogen peroxide and comes into contact with _____, which is found in blood, it results in a new highly energized compound. _____ energy is then released in the form of a blue-green glow. Although potentially helpful to investigators, luminol can also _____ blood samples.

I f you were to put on a white glove and plunge your hand into a tub of black ink, you'd naturally expect the result to be a wet, black glove. But what if you first covered your hand with a strange man-made material
5 known as frozen smoke? You'd end up with a dry hand and a white glove.

Frozen smoke's proper name is "aerogel," and it was created by Steven Kistler in 1931 in an attempt to win a bet that he could replace the liquid inside of a jar with gas without causing
10 any shrinkage. Kistler won the bet and, in the process, discovered aerogel. However, the fragility of the material, along with the costly and difficult manufacturing process it required, hampered widespread production until recently.

Aerogel is semi-transparent, bluish-white and dry to the touch, with a texture similar to that of foam. Structurally, it is extremely porous, which means it is full of
15 small holes. Because of this, it's incredibly lightweight: If you were to try to lift a chunk of aerogel the size of a person, you'd find that it weighs less than a pound. Despite this, it is strong enough to hold more than 2,000 times its own weight, although if enough pressure is applied, it will shatter like glass.

Although aerogel is a solid material, it is made up of up to 99.8 percent air. It can
20 be produced from a variety of chemicals by removing the liquid from a gel and replacing it with gas. Commercially speaking, the most significant characteristic of aerogel is its insulating ability. Aerogel is effective at blocking sound and electricity, but its thermal insulation properties have the most promising applications.

It has already been used to insulate the Rover, a robotic probe that was sent to Mars.
25 During the mission, the temperature on Mars dropped as low as −67 degrees Celsius, but aerogel kept the sensitive electronic components inside of Rover warm and functioning. Another potential usage of aerogel is as a substitute for glass in windows. Because it has 20 times the insulating ability of standard glass, aerogel windows could save homeowners money by minimizing heat loss. It can be employed in various other ways, too, making
30 aerogel a truly versatile material.

WORD
CHECK

Choose the correct words for the blanks from the highlighted words in the passage.

1. to prevent progress or hinder: _____

2. a reduction in size, quality or value: _____

3. a vehicle or machine used for exploration: _____

4. to prevent the passage of heat, electricity, or sound: _____

1 **What is the best title for the passage?**
   a. Aerogel: A Future Alternative to Glass
   b. Aerogel: Too Unstable to Use in Daily Life
   c. Aerogel: An Unusual, Multi-purpose Material
   d. Aerogel: A Heavy, Powerful Insulating Material

2 **Aerogel was first created in an attempt to replace _____.**

3 **Which is NOT mentioned as a reason why aerogel hasn't been used widely?**
   a. fragile makeup
   b. high price to produce
   c. difficult manufacturing process
   d. ability to easily change into liquid

4 **Which is closest in meaning to versatile?**
   a. raw   b. delicate   c. remarkable   d. adaptable

5 **Which is NOT true about aerogel according to the passage?**
   a. It usually exists as a foam.
   b. It is extremely light relative to its size.
   c. It can be made from various chemicals.
   d. It is effective at reducing heat loss.

SUMMARY

6 **Use the words in the box to fill in the blanks.**

produce	heavy	air	strong	insulating	solid	replace

Aerogel is a substance that can _____ the liquid inside a container with gas without causing any shrinkage. Although it was discovered in 1931, aerogel wasn't commonly used until recently because of several problems. This porous, blue-white substance is extremely lightweight but is _____ enough to hold more than 2,000 times its own weight. Though almost totally consisting of _____, the most promising use for aerogel is as an _____ material. This multi-use material has already been employed in a space probe and might one day replace windows in homes.

Survival in the wild can hinge on the ability to remain unseen. Many species of animals accomplish this through camouflage, whether the purpose is to conceal themselves from predators or to sneak up on prey. In either case, the effectiveness of this concealment is often based on an animal's ability to blend into its natural habitat.

5 Blending in can be accomplished through adopting a color that resembles the surrounding environment. For example, deer are the reddish-brown color of the earth around them, whereas sharks are a bluish-gray color, matching the hue of the sea. Other animals utilize pattern or texture to disguise themselves either within their environment or among large same-species groups. Tigers, for example, are striped so as to blend into 10 the tall grasslands they roam in search of food. The stripes of zebras, however, work quite differently. When zebras herd together, their black and white stripes serve as a visual disruption; that is, they make it very difficult for a predator to single out one animal among many.

The method by which animals adapt their colors to their environment depends on 15 physiology. Birds and mammals are generally covered in fur or feathers, which cannot change color; thus there's the need to grow a new coat. Some species, on the other hand, are able to change the appearance of their skin through cells that determine coloration, known as chromatophores. Cuttlefish, for example, manipulate skin cells to change colors and patterns, and marine snails alter their color to match their environment by 20 changing their diet.

Another type of camouflage is known as mimicry. Some species of insects use mimicry to appear to be an inanimate object or even a different kind of animal. When predators approach stick insects, for example, they stand still and are often mistaken for twigs. And, hawk moth caterpillars scare away predators with a pattern on their back that 25 resembles a snake's head. A predator that might want to eat a caterpillar probably wouldn't choose to attack a snake.

Each of these camouflaging devices was developed gradually through the process of natural selection. An animal that _____(A)_____ than other members of its species 30 has a better chance of surviving, and therefore has the opportunity to reproduce and ensure that its genes are passed on to the next generation.

Choose the correct words for the blanks from the highlighted words in the passage.

1. the practice of imitation: _____
2. to group together in large numbers: _____
3. an animal that lives by preying on other animals: _____
4. the act of blending into natural surroundings: _____

1 What is the best title for the passage?

    a. Surviving in the Wild through Camouflage

    b. Animals' Amazing Ability to Change Shape

    c. Species Evolution through Natural Selection

    d. Animals Living in Harmony with the Environment

2 Which is NOT mentioned as a method of camouflage?

    a. utilizing patterns on bodies

    b. producing a new coat of fur or feathers

    c. pretending to be an inanimate object

    d. reflecting light to produce different colors

3 How do hawk moth caterpillars protect themselves from predators?

    _____

4 What is the best expression for blank (A)?

    a. is faster and stronger   b. is more difficult to see

    c. is more colorful and fancier   d. has a greater chance of grabbing prey

5 Which of the following is NOT true according to the passage?

    a. Deer are a reddish-brown color that resembles the earth.

    b. The patterns of zebras help them blend into grasslands.

    c. Cuttlefish change their skin color with their special cells.

    d. Marine snails change their color depending on what they eat.

SUMMARY

6 Fill in the blanks to complete the topic of each paragraph.

    a. Paragraph 1: animals' use of camouflage

    b. Paragraph 2: ways to _____

    c. Paragraph 3: _____

    d. Paragraph 4: _____ as a means of defense

    e. Paragraph 5: _____ in camouflage

The Venus Flytrap

The Venus flytrap is a small, carnivorous plant that grows only in the wetlands of the southeastern United States. The plant's odd name, thought to be a reference to the Roman goddess of love, was chosen by botanists who compared the plant's ability to trap insects to a beautiful woman's ability to ensnare men.

5 It is, in fact, the Venus flytrap's predatory nature that makes it stand out in the world of botany. Although the plants are able to synthesize glucose through photosynthesis, the marshy soil in which they grow lacks other essential nutrients, such as nitrogen. Venus flytraps make up for this deficiency by consuming live prey, such as insects and spiders.

Because Venus flytraps don't have brains and muscles like most carnivores, they 10 rely on a series of mechanical and chemical processes. The plants attract their prey into their traps – specially formed leaves that resemble an open mouth – with sweet-smelling nectar. These leaves are covered in sensitive "trigger hairs." When an insect touches one of them, the plant is alerted to its presence. If a trigger hair is touched for a second time in quick succession, the leaf responds by closing partly shut, trapping the insect with stiff 15 *protuberances that interlock to form a cage.

The trap, however, will not completely close unless the trigger hairs are activated again. ■ This is how the plant differentiates between live prey and other objects that may fall onto its leaves. ■ If the trigger hairs are not reactivated, the leaves slowly open again, an effort that takes about 12 hours, allowing the unwanted object to fall free. ■ This process 20 is designed to allow the plant to avoid wasting precious energy attempting to digest something inedible. ■

Once the leaves have sealed completely shut, trapping the insect inside, the plant begins to feed by producing acidic liquids that act like the digestive fluids in an animal's stomach. The prey is slowly dissolved over the course of the next several days, and its 25 nutrients are absorbed by the plant. Once the nutrients are gone, the trap reopens and the remains are allowed to fall away. When the next unsuspecting creature stumbles into the trap, the process will begin again.

*protuberance: something that extends outward

---

1 The word ensnare in the passage is closest in meaning to

   ⓐ assist   ⓑ capture   ⓒ influence   ⓓ encounter

2 According to paragraph 2, why do Venus flytraps consume insects and spiders?

      ⓐ They cannot rely on photosynthesis year round.

      ⓑ They cannot produce glucose without live prey.

      ⓒ They require nutrients not present in the surrounding soil.

      ⓓ They can easily get them in the surrounding environment.

3 The word them in the passage refers to

      ⓐ Venus flytraps   ⓑ traps   ⓒ insects   ⓓ trigger hairs

4 Look at the four squares [■] that indicate where the following sentence could be added to the passage.

An inanimate twig or leaf, for example, will not reactivate the hairs.

Where would the sentence best fit?

5 Why does the author mention an animal's stomach in paragraph 5?

      ⓐ To describe the motion of a prey

      ⓑ To explain how flytraps absorb nutrients

      ⓒ To suggest that flytraps are not really plants

      ⓓ To compare flytraps and animal feeding processes

6   Directions   An introductory sentence for a brief summary of the passage is provided below. Complete the summary by selecting the THREE answer choices that express the most important ideas in the passage.

The Venus flytrap of the southeastern U.S. is unique in the plant world in that it is carnivorous.

      ⓐ Botanists named the plant after the Roman goddess of love, Venus.

      ⓑ The flytrap's predatory nature is the result of certain environmental limitations.

      ⓒ The leaves of Venus flytraps are covered with tiny hairs that alert them to the presence of prey.

      ⓓ A series of processes involving their leaves allows flytraps to trap prey and avoid unwanted materials.

      ⓔ Flytraps dissolve their prey with acid to acquire needed nutrients.

      ⓕ It can take several days for a flytrap to break down its prey before releasing the remains.

An ombudsman is an official who serves as a liaison between the public and an organization by receiving and investigating complaints. The odd-sounding title comes from the Swedish language but has been adopted into standard English. The first modern official ombudsmen were appointed by the Swedish government early in the 19th century, although similar positions existed in a variety of cultures around the world.

Ombudsmen traditionally serve a political role, acting as representatives of common citizens who have complaints against their elected officials. Although ombudsmen are appointed by the government as opposed to being elected by the people, they maintain their impartiality by operating independently outside of the system. They generally don't have the power to take legal action against the government if evidence of wrongdoing is found, but they can bring the situation under investigation by publishing a report on their findings. Whenever possible, they seek to resolve situations before they go to the courts.

These days, however, the position of ombudsman is also being utilized in a variety of non-governmental institutions, such as universities, private businesses, hospitals, and nonprofit organizations. It is critical that organizational ombudsmen remain impartial. They are charged primarily with safeguarding the legal and ethical interests of company employees. They also monitor new issues that may affect their employers, addressing them before they can cause problems. Organizational ombudsmen are high-ranking officials but are not part of the company's management, often reporting to a board of directors.

The news ombudsman is another non-governmental variation of the position, usually employed by media outlets. The position provides the public with an avenue for their complaints and keeps journalists in touch with the public's views. News ombudsmen listen to complaints about the accuracy and balance of news stories and then present suggestions to the journalists and editors involved. By doing so, they ensure that future news coverage will be fair and balanced, while encouraging readers or viewers by allowing them to have their say.

It has become increasingly apparent that ombudsmen can play an important role in any sort of organization that deals with the public, providing citizens with not only an ear for their complaints but also a voice.

WORD CHECK

Choose the correct words for the blanks from the highlighted words in the passage.

1. extremely important: _____
2. being unbiased or fair: _____
3. exposure given by the media: _____
4. a coordinator of communication between groups: _____

1   What is the main idea of the passage?
    a. Ombudsmen fight against the power of institutions.
    b. The public has a right to elect their own representatives.
    c. Many organizations work with the law to deal with the public's issues.
    d. Ombudsmen help people make their complaints and concerns known.

2   How do ombudsmen keep their impartiality while serving a political role?

    _____

3   Which is NOT mentioned as a role of organizational ombudsmen?
    a. protecting the legal and ethical interests of employees
    b. checking new issues related to their employers
    c. resolving conflicts between employers and employees
    d. making reports to a board of directors

4   According to the passage, news ombudsmen _____.
    a. help journalists find correct information
    b. immediately reply to complaints concerning news
    c. give appropriate suggestions to correct or clarify news reports
    d. write articles about the rights of readers or viewers

5   Which of the following is NOT true according to the passage?
    a. The term "ombudsman" comes from the Swedish language.
    b. The role of ombudsman was officially created early in the 19th century.
    c. Ombudsmen serve a political role on behalf of common citizens.
    d. Ombudsmen enforce the law to prevent improper government activity.

SUMMARY

6   Fill in the blanks to complete the topic of each paragraph.
    a. Paragraph 1: _____ to the term ombudsman
    b. Paragraph 2: _____ of ombudsmen
    c. Paragraph 3: _____
    d. Paragraph 4: _____
    e. Paragraph 5: _____ to society

Populism generally refers to political activities or ideals that claim to promote the interests of the public. Often, populism is understood to be a political party's strategy of utilizing the public's interests to its advantage as a means to gain or maintain power. The term populism originated from the Populist Party, or the People's Party, which was first organized in the U.S. in 1891. It came up with mass appeal policies to compete against other parties. This strategy later came to be known as a typical characteristic of populism.

Argentina's former presidential couple, Juan and Eva Peron, are well-known examples of populists. Juan Peron, who was elected president on a wave of public support after World War II, adopted pro-labor policies to maintain his power. He also provided unlimited material support to the public, justifying his policies as being reformative. Meanwhile, his wife, Eva Peron, was revered as the "mother of Argentina." She acted cold-heartedly toward the rich and was kind and charitable to the poor. But as a result of their radical reforms, Argentina fell deep into debt and faced abrupt economic ruin. Having been a top five world economic power until the 1940s, Argentina is still struggling today from the consequences of populism.

Behind the policies of populism always lies _____(A)_____. Populists often adopt paternalistic attitudes by having direct dialogues with the public and presenting their ideas through writing. They also attack the privileges of the rich and the powerful while appealing to the middle and lower classes with their anti-elitist ideals. That is why they often employ policies that prioritize the distribution of wealth.

At first glance, there seems to be nothing wrong with populist policies, since they appear to benefit the public. However, policies that call for extreme distribution of wealth can cause tremendous financial loss and inflation. This leads to a vicious cycle of low growth, causing lower wages for the public and ultimately threatening the national economy.

All around the globe, many politicians are still relying on populist sentiment to gain support. Hopefully, behind the rhetoric lies the wisdom to turn popular support for policies into a foundation for national growth, instead of allowing it to be utilized as a means to seize political power.

WORD CHECK

Choose the correct words for the blanks from the highlighted words in the passage.

1. to put things in order of importance or urgency: _____

2. a persuasive style of speech that flatters or deceives: _____

3. wanting to help or advise but often being overprotective: _____

4. changing to a better state or amending what is wrong or corrupt: _____

1 **What is the best title for the passage?**
   a. The Collapse of Populism
   b. Heroes of Argentina, the Perons
   c. The Hidden Hazards of Populist Policies
   d. Populism, the Potential Benefits to the Public

2 **What was the result of Juan Peron's policies?**

_____

3 **What is the best expression for blank (A)?**
   a. a genuine effort to help the public
   b. the intention to acquire public support
   c. a strategy to compete with other parties
   d. the purpose of developing the country's economy

4 **Which is NOT true about populists according to the passage?**
   a. They act based on public support.
   b. They adopt policies that benefit the entire public.
   c. They often use the tool of writing to gain mass appeal.
   d. Their policies of extreme wealth distribution can threaten the national economy.

SUMMARY

5 **Fill in the blanks to complete the topic of each paragraph.**
   a. Paragraph 1: _____
   b. Paragraph 2: _____
   c. Paragraph 3: _____
   d. Paragraph 4: _____
   e. Paragraph 5: hope for populism to be used wisely

In an ideal legal system, all criminals would be immediately brought to court and punished for their offenses. But in reality, there are laws that actually free criminals from the burden of being brought to

5 court for their crimes _____(A)_____.
Tracing their roots back to Roman times, these laws are known as "statutes of limitations."

The expiration periods set by statutes of limitations vary depending on the types of cases, and there are certain case types that are not covered by such statutes. In most

10 states in the U.S., there is no statute of limitations for murder cases, and the right to file lawsuits against murder suspects never expires. However, in many countries, statutes of limitations apply even to murder cases. Each country sets different expiration periods for murder; for example, it is 25 years in Korea and 30 years in Taiwan.

Advocates of statutes of limitations claim there are valid reasons why lawmakers

15 enacted these laws. One purpose of statutes of limitations is to maintain fairness. In other words, memories fade, evidence can be damaged, and witnesses disappear with the passing of time, making circumstances unsuitable for court trials. Another reason for statutes of limitations is closure or certainty, meaning society and law enforcement agencies will eventually stop investing effort and public resources in trying to investigate

20 old cases that are unlikely to be resolved, and instead turn their attention to recent crimes.

Opponents of statutes of limitations see them as an irrelevance and call for the legal system to be updated accordingly. They point, first, to advances in scientific investigation. Modern techniques used in evidence recovery and analysis mean that a crime can be proven long after it was committed. Secondly, they believe that certain crimes should

25 never be sent to the unsolved file and that criminals should be made to pay for their crimes no matter what the circumstances are. Allowing the perpetrators of murder or child rape to escape unpunished, they argue, may even encourage such criminal behavior.

Whether legally or morally justifiable, statutes of limitations must at the very least reflect social interest. Lawmakers must remain mindful of the fact that punishment is a

30 tool of social order, but that so too is faith in the law.

WORD CHECK

Choose the correct words for the blanks from the highlighted words in the passage.

1. an illegal act or a crime: _____

2. the end of an official period: _____

3. sth unrelated to a matter being considered: _____

4. a legal case between two parties in a court of law: _____

1 **What is the best title for the passage?**
   a. Is the Law Equal for Everybody?
   b. Do Crimes Have Expiration Dates?
   c. Does Every Case Possess Valid Evidence?
   d. Do Criminals Have the Right to Be Protected?

2 **What is the best expression for blank (A)?**
   a. when they confess
   b. when sufficient evidence is not obtained
   c. once a certain amount of time has passed
   d. if they plead self-defense

3 **What is LEAST likely to be said by advocates of statutes of limitations?**
   a. There is a possibility of discovering errors in people's memories.
   b. Damaged evidence can confuse judgment.
   c. Old cases can be solved with recent scientific techniques.
   d. We can't handle old cases because public resources are limited.

4 **Why do opponents of statutes of limitations worry about having criminals go unpunished?**

   _____

5 **Which of the following is NOT true according to the passage?**
   a. The statute of limitations period depends on case types.
   b. In the U.S., the statutes of limitations don't apply to murder cases in most states.
   c. Most countries have statutes of limitations only for less serious offenses.
   d. A criminal who committed murder 30 years ago cannot be punished in Korea.

SUMMARY

6 **Use the words in the box to fill in the blanks.**

| scientific   arrest   techniques   unsolvable   responsible   fairness   perpetrators |

Due to laws known as statutes of limitations, criminals are no longer _____ for certain crimes after a set period of time has passed. The purpose of these laws is to maintain _____, as witnesses and evidence become unreliable over time. They also relieve investigators from the burden of having to concentrate on older crimes. Opponents, however, say that modern police _____ mean that evidence can still be gathered years later. They also believe that no crime should be considered _____.

Trial by Jury

In the U.S., as in many countries around the world, accused criminals are tried under a jury system. A panel of ordinary citizens is charged with hearing the facts in a case and delivering a verdict. A judge presides over the trial to ensure that all appropriate laws and rules of conduct are followed, but he or she does not interfere with the jury's decision.

5 Variations of this concept have been implemented since ancient times, but an early version of the modern jury system was introduced by the Magna Carta, an English document granting certain people the right to be tried before a group of their peers.

A jury is made up of individual jurors, in most instances numbering 12. The jurors listen to the testimonies and arguments presented by both the defense and prosecution,

10 consider these facts, and agree on a verdict of either guilty or not guilty. Different situations dictate different requirements for reaching a verdict, ranging from a simple majority to a unanimous decision by the jury.

American jurors are chosen at random from lists of registered voters and licensed drivers. However, many people are excluded from jury duty – those whose jobs do not

15 allow them to take the time to serve on a jury and people with medical conditions, criminal records, or conflicting religious beliefs. Potential jurors must also be examined to verify their lack of bias and outside interest in the case before they are accepted by the defense and prosecution.

■ During the trial, jurors are forbidden from obtaining any information about the case

20 outside of the trial setting. ■ Once the trial is concluded, the jury assembles to deliberate on a verdict in the case. ■ There is no set time limit for deliberations, and American criminal trials require a unanimous decision, so juries have been known to take days to reach a verdict. ■

The jury system is seen as a vital part of democratic government, as it allows ordinary

25 people to take part in the administration of justice. Because the selection process is random, juries represent a diverse and accurate sampling of local populations. In this way, the criminal justice system is integrally connected to the community, not above or at odds with it.

---

1 The author mentions the Magna Carta in paragraph 1 in order to

ⓐ describe how justice systems have developed

ⓑ compare and contrast English and American juries

ⓒ identify an early version of the modern jury system

ⓓ suggest that judges had more power in previous centuries

2 According to paragraph 2, jurors must do all of the following EXCEPT

(a) hear arguments from both the defense and prosecution

(b) report on their decision-making process

(c) review statements presented in the case

(d) make a judgment of guilt or innocence

3 The word verify in the passage is closest in meaning to

(a) confirm   (b) approve   (c) present   (d) question

4 Look at the four squares [■] that indicate where the following sentence could be added to the passage.

This allows them to focus solely on the facts that are presented by the defense and prosecution.

Where would the sentence best fit?

5 The word it in the passage refers to

(a) jury system

(b) democratic government

(c) administration of justice

(d) selection process

6 Directions   An introductory sentence for a brief summary of the passage is provided below. Complete the summary by selecting the THREE answer choices that express the most important ideas in the passage.

In the American system of justice, it is up to a jury to try some legal cases.

(a) The judge holds an important position during a trial, but the jury alone is responsible for reaching a verdict.

(b) Most juries are made up of 12 members, but the number can range according to the situation.

(c) Jurors attend the trial to hear testimonies and evaluate guilt.

(d) There are some people in society who are exempt from serving on a jury.

(e) Jurors have to remain unbiased and free from outside influence during a trial.

(f) In a democracy, the jury system enables citizens to participate directly in the administration of justice.

WORD REVIEW TEST

[1~3] Choose the word that is closest in meaning to the underlined one.

1. Patrick explained the concept in <u>minute</u> detail, so I understood it easily.
   a. tiny   b. valid   c. vivid   d. rough

2. Journalists are required to provide factual information with <u>impartiality</u>.
   a. sentiment   b. variation   c. judgement   d. fairness

3. Buddhism affirms that all life must be <u>revered</u>.
   a. struggled   b. approved   c. respected   d. protected

[4~7] Connect each phrase in column B with its matching verb in column A.

A		B
4. reach •		• a. a law
5. enact •		• b. a lawsuit
6. release •		• c. excess energy
7. file •		• d. a verdict

[8~12] Choose the best word to complete each sentence. (Change the form if needed.)

> insulate   versatile   deliberate   differentiate   manipulate   disguise   hamper

8. Rescue work was _____ by heavy rains.

9. The government is _____ whether to pass the law.

10. If water pipes aren't _____, they can freeze and burst in winter.

11. The criminal _____ himself as a woman so nobody would recognize him.

12. A chameleon has the ability to _____ its colors.

[13~16] Choose the correct word for each definition.

> unanimous   inedible   rhetoric   deficiency   vicious   porous

13. full of holes:

14. a lack or shortage of sth:

15. agreed upon by all:

16. not fit to eat:

[17~22] Choose the best word to complete each sentence.

17. I _____ the tasks considering the importance of each.

    a. ensnare   b. shatter   c. accelerate   d. prioritize

18. Margarine is a good _____ for butter.

    a. liaison   b. substitute   c. nutrient   d. compound

19. I have to renew my passport because it _____ soon.

    a. expires   b. dictates   c. forbids   d. functions

20. A referee should be completely without _____.

    a. bias   b. closure   c. asset   d. administration

21. A lie detector detects _____ or lies.

    a. fragility   b. coverage   c. irrelevance   d. concealment

22. Crimes such as murder and rape are major _____.

    a. offenses   b. disruptions   c. testimonies   d. perpetrators

[23~25] Circle the odd one out in each group.

23. emit   conceal   release   give off
24. hazard   threat   risk   trap
25. rely on   take on   hinge on   depend on

[26] Read and write the right number of the correct definition for each sentence.

> **charge** *v.* **1.** to ask someone for a certain amount of money for something: *The restaurant charged us 40 dollars for the wine.* **2.** to state officially that someone is guilty of a crime: *The man the police arrested last night has been charged with murder.* **3.** to make someone responsible for something: *The commission is charged with inspecting the national budget.*

    a. Christina was charged with stealing the jewels. _____
    b. The WTO is charged with promoting an international trade system. _____

ADVANCED
READING
EXPERT

A HIGH-LEVEL READING COURSE for TOP-RANKING EFL Readers

1

NE _ Neungyule

Answers & Explanations

ADVANCED
READING
EXPERT

A HIGH-LEVEL READING COURSE for TOP-RANKING EFL Readers

1

Answers & Explanations

UNIT 01.
Food

READING 1
p. 8~9

WORD CHECK

1. consumption   2. enhance   3. restricted
4. processed
▶ neurological: related to the brain and nervous system

정답

1. c   2. a. MSG b. high fructose corn syrup c.
aspartame   3. b   4. Eat home cooked meals. / Read
the food labels. / Buy organic products.   5. artificial,
weight, full, natural

해석

　　오늘날 구입할 수 있는 식품 대부분은 화학 약품 및 가공 물질로 가득
하다. '첨가물'이라고 불리는 그것은 식품에 풍미를 더하고 식감을 좋게 하
거나, 유통기한을 늘리기 위해 사용되고 있다. 하지만 가장 흔히 쓰이고 있
는 첨가제 중 일부는 심각한 건강 문제를 야기하는 것으로 드러나고 있다.

　　가장 흔한 식품 첨가물 중 하나인 아스파르템은 '다이어트'와 '무설탕'
이라고 붙여진 식품에 사용되는 인공 감미료이다. 연구들이 이 물질과 다양
한 유형의 암, 당뇨, 불안감 및 여러 다른 질병 및 상태를 연관지어왔다. 이
물질은 아주 다양한 음식에서 찾아볼 수 있는데, 다이어트 및 무설탕 탄산
음료, 무설탕 껌, 구취 제거 민트, 다양한 후식, 치약, 그리고 심지어 씹어 먹
는 비타민에도 들어있다!

　　또 다른 위험한 인공 감미료는 액상과당이다. 이것은 '나쁜' 콜레스테롤
인 LDL 수치를 증가시키고, 신체 조직을 손상시키며, 사람들의 체중을 증
가시킨다. 놀랍게도, 이 물질이 거의 모든 가공 식품에 사용되고 있기 때문
에 이것은 많은 사람들의 주요 열량 공급원 중 하나가 되었다.

　　글루탐산소다, 즉 MSG는 수프, 샐러드 드레싱, 과자, 냉동식품 등의
맛을 증진시키기 위해 사용된다. 이 물질이 포만감을 느끼게 하는 뇌의 신경
통로를 차단하기 때문에, 이로 인해 많은 사람들이 과식을 하게 된다. MSG
는 또한 심각하게 세포를 손상시키며, 정기적으로 이 첨가제를 섭취하는 것
이 우울증, 시력 손상, 피로감 및 두통과 연관이 있다는 연구가 나오고 있다.

　　마지막으로 패스트푸드, 마가린 및 다른 가공 식품에 들어있는 트랜스
지방 또한 음식 천연의 맛을 증진시켜준다. 하지만 이것은 LDL 콜레스테
롤 수치를 높일 뿐만 아니라, '좋은' 콜레스테롤인 HDL 수치를 낮춘다. 이
물질은 당뇨병에서부터 심장병까지 모든 종류의 건강 문제와 연관되어지고
있다. 이 물질은 실제로 너무 위험하다고 여겨져 덴마크, 아이슬란드, 스웨
덴 같은 나라에서는 요즘 엄격히 제한되거나 금지되고 있다.

　　유감스럽게도 식품 첨가물은 너무 흔해졌기 때문에 피하기가 어렵다.
하지만 더 건강하게 먹기 위해 할 수 있는 일이 몇 가지 있다. 패스트푸드나
가공 식품을 먹기 보다는 가능한 자주 집에서 요리한 음식을 먹어라. 그리
고 식료품을 살 때, 그 식품에 포함된 성분과 첨가물이 나열된 식품 라벨을
읽는 것을 기억하라. 마지막으로 가능한 한 많이 유기농 제품을 구입하라.
더 자주 천연의 무첨가 식품을 먹을수록 더 건강해질 것이다!

구문 해설

(1행)　Much of the food [that is available today] is full of
chemicals and processed substances.
　▶ [ ]은 Much of the food를 수식하는 주격관계대명사절이다.

(5행)　Aspartame, ..., is an artificial sweetener [**used** in
foods [that are labeled "diet" and "sugar free]]."
　▶ used 이하는 an artificial sweetener를 수식하는 과거분사
구이다.

(20행)　However, **not only** *does* it increase levels of LDL
cholesterol, **but** it **also** decreases ...
　▶ 〈Not only V + S, but S + also +V〉 구문은 주어와 동사의
어순에 주의한다.

(31행)　**The more often** you eat natural, whole foods, **the
healthier** you will be!
　▶ the 비교급 ~, the 비교급 ...: ~하면 할수록 더욱 …하다

READING 2
p. 10~11

WORD CHECK

1. inhibit   2. hazard   3. dehydration   4. additive
▶ stimulation: an act of making sth begin to work

정답

1. b   2. They target students, athletes and anyone else
who wants an extra energy kick.   3. b   4. c   5. c
6. a - ②, b - ③, c - ①, d - ⑤, e - ④

해석

　　사람들은 왜 탄산음료를 마시는가? 아마도 탄산음료가 맛이 좋다고 생
각하기 때문일 것이다. 하지만 최근 탄산음료 시장은 맛을 넘어 효능이 있
다고 주장하는 제품들로 넘쳐나고 있다. 에너지 음료는 이렇게 탄산음료 시
장에 새롭게 등장한 것들 중 하나이다. 이름에서 알 수 있듯이, 에너지 음료
는 에너지를 증강시켜 준다고 주장한다. 에너지 음료는 학생, 운동 선수 및
에너지 증강을 원하는 그 밖의 모든 사람들을 위해 고안되었다. 그러나 그
것들이 신체에 미치는 진정한 효과에 대한 우려들이 있다.

　　에너지 음료는 단기간에 신체적 및 정신적 자극을 유발한다. 하지만 이
것은 에너지 음료에 각종 비타민과 건강 첨가물이 함유되어 있기 때문이 아
니다. 마시는 사람이 느끼는 실제 효능은 순전히 설탕과 카페인의 혼합에
서 기인하는 것이다. 에너지 음료 한 개에는 일반적으로 탄산음료 캔 한 개
보다 두 배 이상의 카페인이 함유되어 있다. 카페인은 잠을 유발하는 아데
노신의 생성을 억제하고, 사람의 정신을 맑게 할 수 있는 아드레날린과 도
파민을 증가시킨다.

　　그러므로 에너지 음료를 마시는 것의 위험성은 커피를 마시는 것의 위
험성과 거의 같다. 어떤 사람들은 심장 박동수 증가, 불안감, 수면 장애를
호소한다. 그리고 카페인은 중독성이 있기 때문에 에너지 음료 소비자들
은 많은 대형 에너지 음료 제조업체들의 제품 라벨에 표시되어 있는 대로

하루 최대 500ml의 권장량을 지키는 게 어렵다는 것을 알게 될 수도 있다.

　신체 운동 중 몸에 수분을 보충하는 데 도움을 주는 스포츠 음료와는 달리, 에너지 음료는 실제로 이뇨제 역할을 하며, 그렇게 함으로써 몸이 보유하고 있는 물의 양을 감소시킨다. 따라서 장기간의 운동 중에 에너지 음료를 마시면 위험할 수 있음은 알기 쉽다. 그러나 잠재된 위험은 탈수의 위험을 넘어선다. 일부 에너지 음료에는 효능이 아직 충분히 검증되지 않은 다른 성분들과 더불어 심장 질환과 연관있고 살 빼는 약들에 흔히 사용되는 흥분제인 에페드린도 함유되어 있다.

　적당히 사용되면 에너지 음료는 활기없는 사람들에게 안전한 자극원이 될 수 있다. 그러나 우리가 몸 속에 무엇을 집어넣고 있는지 그리고 그것이 끼칠 수 있는 영향을 정확하게 이해하는 것이 중요하다.

구문 해설

12행 A single energy drink typically contains more than **twice as** much caffeine **as** a can of soda.
▶ 배수사 + as + 원급 + as ~: ~의 …배인

15행 The risks of consuming energy drinks **are**, therefore, roughly **the same as** *those* of drinking coffee.
▶ be the same as ~: ~와 똑같다
▶ those는 The risks의 중복을 피하기 위해 사용된 지시대명사이다.

17행 ..., energy drink consumers may find **it** difficult **to limit** themselves ... per day **as** (it is) indicated on ...
▶ it은 to limit ... per day를 진목적어로 하는 가목적어이다.
▶ as는 양태의 접속사로 '~ 대로'의 의미를 지닌다.

25행 ... ephedrine, a stimulant [often used in diet pills [that has been linked to heart problems]], along with other ingredients [whose effects are ...].

UNIT 02.
Economy

READING 1
p. 12~13

WORD CHECK

1. optimal　2. associated with　3. mansion　4. mow
▶ efficient: able to work without wasting time

정답

1. a　2. d　3. It refers to what we lose when we decide on a certain action.　4. d　5. c　6. decide, absolute, higher, lose

---

해석

　개개인은 그들이 잘하는 무언가에 집중해야 한다. 예를 들어, 훌륭한 배우들은 그들의 시간을 영화를 촬영하는 데 헌신해야 한다. 그렇지 않는 것은 그들의 재능을 낭비하는 것이다. 하지만 사람들은 다른 일에도 능숙할 수 있다. 예를 들어 배우가 특히 잔디를 잘 깎는다고 하자. 그렇다고 그가 자신의 저택 주변의 엄청난 잔디를 스스로 깎아야 하는 것일까? 절대우위, 기회비용과 비교우위라는 경제 용어를 살펴보는 것이 이 질문에 대한 답을 하는 데 도움을 줄 수도 있다.

　그 배우가 4시간 안에 잔디를 깎을 수 있고, 같은 일을 하는 데 이웃의 10대 남자아이는 8시간이 걸릴 것이라고 가정해 보자. 그들의 생산성을 비교하면 같은 결과를 내기 위해 절반만 투입하면 되기 때문에 그 배우가 10대 남자아이보다 절대우위에 있다고 경제학자들은 말할 것이다. 즉, 일을 하기 위해 필요한 시간의 양을 고려했을 때 그 배우가 더 효율적인 것이다. 하지만 그의 시간의 가치도 또한 참작되어야 한다.

　그 4시간 동안 배우는 TV 광고를 찍고 50,000달러를 벌 수 있다. 이 잠재적인 수입은 광고를 찍는 대신 잔디를 깎기로 선택한 것에 대한 배우의 기회비용이다. 기회비용의 개념은 어떤 행위를 하겠다고 결정했을 때 잃게 되는 것을 말한다. 어떤 일을 하는 것이 그 행동과 연관된 손실을 감수할 만한지를 결정할 때 기회비용은 고려되어야 한다. 그 10대 아이가 패스트푸드 점에서 8시간 일해서 80달러밖에 벌지 못한다면 배우가 잃게 되는 것보다 훨씬 적게 잃는 것이다.

　이러한 기회비용의 비교가 누가 잔디를 깎아야 하는지를 결정하는 열쇠이다. 이렇게 비교우위가 계산되는 것이다. 이 개념에 따르면 기회비용이 적은 사람이 비교우위를 가지게 되고 그 행위를 해야 하는 것이다. 이 경우에는 10대 아이가 80달러 이상을 벌고 그 배우가 50,000달러 이하의 비용이 드는 한 10대 아이에게 비교우위가 있는 것이다.

　그 배우가 광고를 찍는 동안 남자아이가 잔디를 깎도록 고용한다면 10대 아이와 배우 모두에게 이익이 될 것이다. 마찬가지로 정부는 무역에서 오는 최적의 이익을 결정하기 위해 여러 나라의 제품을 살펴볼 때 기회비용과 비교우위를 고려한다. 이렇게 함으로써 모든 국가가 다른 나라와 상품을 무역하면서 이익을 얻을 수 있도록 보장하는 것이다.

구문 해설

9행 ... it would **take** a teenage boy from his neighborhood eight hours **to do** the same job.
▶ take + 사람 + 시간 + to-v: ~가 …하는 데 (시간)이 걸리다

12행 ..., the actor is more efficient when considering the quantity of time [**required** to do the job].
▶ required 이하는 time을 수식하는 과거분사구이다.

22행 This comparison of opportunity cost is **the key to determining** *who should mow the lawn.*
▶ the key to + 명사상당어구: ~의 열쇠
▶ who 이하는 determining의 목적어 역할을 하는 간접의문문으로 '누가 ~하는지'로 해석된다.

24행 ..., **whoever** has the lower opportunity cost has a
　　　　　S　　　　　　　　　　　V₁
comparative advantage and should perform the
　　　　　　　　　　　　　　V₂
action.

▶ whoever는 anyone who와 바꿔쓸 수 있으며 '~하는 사람
은 누구든지'라는 의미로 명사절을 이끌 수 있다.

정답

1. ⓑ   2. ⓓ   3. ⓑ   4. ⓒ   5. The third square
6. General demarketing: ⓓ, ⓕ / Selective demarketing:
ⓑ / Ostensible demarketing: ⓐ, ⓖ

해석

디마케팅

마케팅은 특정 제품이나 서비스에 대한 수요를 창출하고 유지하며 늘
리는 행위로 정의될 수 있다. 그러나 기업들이 이와 같은 수요를 억제하려
고 하는 특정 시나리오들이 존재한다. 이런 경우 '디마케팅'이라고 알려져
있는 방법이 사용된다.

일반적으로 말하면, 디마케팅은 세 가지 범주로 나뉠 수 있는데, 그 첫
번째는 일반적 디마케팅이라고 알려져 있다. 이것은 모든 사용자들을 대상
으로 제품의 수요가 억제될 때 발생하는데, 이때는 정부가 국민들에게 휘
발유나 전기와 같은 자원의 소비를 제한하도록 설득하려고 하는 때인 주로
부족현상의 시기이다. 이것은 또한 제품이 대중의 건강에 위협이 될 것으
로 여겨질 때도 시행된다.

반면에 선택적 디마케팅은 특정 고객층을 대상으로 한다. 기업들은 일
반적으로 이익이 덜 나는 것으로 판명된 고객층에게 선택적 디마케팅을 사
용할 것이다. 이러한 비우량 고객들의 수요는 제한되고, 마케팅 자원은 보
다 이익이 되는 핵심층에 집중된다. 예를 들어, 일부 은행들은 잔고가 많은
고객들에게는 특화된 서비스를 제공하는 반면에 이익이 덜 되는 고객들에
게는 자동입출금기에 줄을 서서 순서를 기다리게 한다.

세 번째 범주인 표면적 디마케팅은 기업이 제품의 매력을 강화하기 위
해 제품의 입수 가능성을 억제하는 상황들이 좋은 예가 된다. 이 유형의 디
마케팅은 흔히 크리스마스 시즌 동안에 최고급 장난감에 적용되는데, 제품
을 구매하는 데 소비자가 직면하는 어려움은 그들의 눈에 그 제품의 가치를
증가시킨다. 그러므로, 실제로 수요는 적어지기 보다는 많아진다.

고급 이미지 창출을 위해 노력하는 일부 기업들은 광고의 범위를 제한
함으로써 제품을 디마케팅한다. 귀금속 기업은 소수의 잡지에만 광고하면
서 자사 제품에 한정성이라는 환상을 심어줄지도 모른다. 이와 유사하게 다
른 기업들은 자사 위스키를 비싼 술집에서만 판매하는 주류 제조업체와 같
이 배급의 범위를 제한함으로써 디마케팅한다. 또 다른 방법은 제품과 관련
된 건강상의 위험성들을 약술하는 경고 라벨을 사용하는 것이다. 담배 회사
들은 그런 라벨을 사용하여 현 사용자들을 일깨우는 동시에 자사가 보다 인
정이 많아 보이도록 만든다. 이런 방법들을 통해 기업들은 고급스러운 브랜
드 이미지를 창출하거나 기업의 이미지를 향상시킬 수 있다.

디마케팅을 단지 마케팅의 반대말 정도로 보는 것은 굉장히 지나친 단
순화일 것이다. 이것은 대중 수요의 흐름을 통제하는 데 도움이 되도록 여
러 상황에서 사용될 수 있는 미묘한 경영 전략이다.

2행 Certain scenarios exist, however, [**in which**
organizations seek to discourage …].
▶ [ ]는 주어 Certain scenarios를 수식하는 〈전치사 + 관계대
명사절〉이다.

16행 The third category, ostensible demarketing, is
exemplified by situations [in which a business
withholds …].

21행 Some companies [that are seeking to create an
upscale image] demarket …
▶ [ ]는 주어 Some companies를 수식하는 주격 관계대명사
절이다.

UNIT 03.
Technology

WORD CHECK

1. attribute   2. convert   3. enrollment
4. authentication
▶ security: actions taken to ensure safety

정답

1. a   2. b - c - d - a   3. (1) the pupil, iris, eyelid,
and eyelashes (2) the shape and location of the vein
structure   4. b   5. d   6. a - ③, b - ②, c - ④, d - ①,
e - ⑤

해석

당신은 비밀번호를 잊어버릴 수도 있고, 열쇠를 엉뚱한 곳에 둘 수도
있지만, 절대 당신 자신을 두고 집을 나가지는 않을 것이다. 암호의 보다 안
전한 대안으로 환영받고 있는 첨단 기술의 생체 인증 시스템이 종래의 보안
장치들을 대체하기 시작하고 있다.

생체 시스템은 독특한 신체적 및 행동적 특징들을 인식함으로써 개인
의 신분을 인증한다. 이 시스템은 자동화되어 있고, 아주 정밀하며, 사용하
는 데 있어 오랜 시간이나 많은 훈련을 필요로 하지 않는다. 종래의 보안 시
스템에 비해 이것의 이점은 분실되거나 쉽게 도난당할 수 있는 요소에 의
존하지 않는다는 것이다.

생체 인증 시스템을 이용하기 위한 첫 번째 단계는 등록이다. 이 단계에
서는 이 시스템을 이용할 각 개인에 대한 기초적인 생체 정보를 탐지하고 수

집하는 센서가 사용된다. 다음으로 이 정보가 수학적 알고리즘으로 전환되어 컴퓨터 데이터베이스에 입력되면서 저장이 이루어진다. 마지막 단계는 비교이다. 관련된 생체 특징들이 검색되고, 그 결과들이 소프트웨어 프로그램을 사용하여 데이터베이스에 저장된 정보와 비교된다. 만일 그것들이 일치하면 그 대상의 신분이 인증되고 접근이 허용된다. 개인의 신분을 확인할 수 있는 다양한 생체 분석들이 있다. 필체가 그 중 하나이다. 대상이 터치패드에 단어를 쓰면 시스템이 필기의 속도, 리듬, 압력, 펜의 각도와 같은 다양한 요소들을 분석한다. 홍채 검사는 또 다른 인기 있는 생체 분석 형태이다. 시스템의 카메라가 눈 사진을 찍은 후 그것이 근적외선을 사용하여 동공, 홍채, 눈꺼풀, 속눈썹을 측정하고 분석함으로써 개인을 인증한다. 생체 측정에 사용되는 또 하나의 독특한 신체적 특성은 정맥 구조이다. 이 시스템은 적외선이 나오는 카메라를 사용하여 정맥 구조의 형태와 위치를 분석한다.

생체 측정법은 종래의 보안 시스템보다 더욱 믿을 만한 신분 증명 수단을 제공한다. 그러나 약간의 사생활과 관련된 문제들이 있다. 일단 생체 정보가 시스템에 등록되었다면, 그것은 다른 곳에 전송되어 본인의 허락도 없이 여러 다른 용도로 사용될 수가 있다. 만약 기술에 정통한 도둑들이 사용자의 생체 ID를 복사할 수 있다면, 개인의 특징은 변경되거나 다시 고쳐질 수 없기 때문에 사용자는 평생토록 문제를 안고 살아야 할지도 모른다. 생체 측정법이 우리 삶의 일상적인 요소가 되려면 이 문제들이 처리되어야 할 것이다.

구문 해설

3행 (Being) **Hailed** as a safer alternative to passcodes, high-tech biometric authentication systems ...
▶ Hailed ... passcodes는 동시동작을 나타내는 수동형 분사구문이다.

11행 This involves the use of a sensor [to detect ... on each individual [**who** will use...]].
▶ who 이하는 each individual을 수식하는 주격 관계대명사절이다.

27행 **Once** the biometric data has been captured by a system, it can potentially ...
▶ once는 접속사로 '일단 ~하면'의 의미이다.

31행 These issues will have to be addressed if biometrics **is to** become an everyday fixture ...
▶ be to-v: (주로 if절 안에서) ~하려면

READING 2

p. 18~19

WORD CHECK

1. a myriad of   2. prank   3. anonymous
4. cumbersome
▶ threat: sth that has the intention to cause harm

1. c   2. d   3. sending anonymous text messages that resemble system-generated warnings   4. a   5. a
6. wireless, radio waves, freedom, ease

해석

덴마크의 Harald Bluetooth 왕은 10세기에 자신의 왕국을 노르웨이와 통일시킴으로써 역사에 이름을 남겼다. 수백 년이 지난 후 새로운 블루투스(Bluetooth)가 무선 기술을 통해 전자 장치를 통합함으로써 자신의 명성을 쌓고 있다.

Harald 왕을 기념하여 이름 지어진 블루투스 기술은 스웨덴 통신사인 Ericsson에 의해 휴대용 컴퓨터, 휴대전화, 디지털 카메라와 같은 휴대용 전자 장치들 간에 성가신 케이블 연결을 제거하기 위한 수단으로 개발되었다. 주로 이런 케이블을 통해 공유되던 데이터는 대신 전파라는 매체를 통해 전달된다. 이 전파는 다른 무선 장치들을 찾아 그에 접속할 때 10m의 거리에까지 전달될 수 있다. 블루투스는 전력을 많이 소비하는 장치가 아니며, 값비싼 하드웨어를 필요로 하지도 않고, 빠르고 쉽게 네트워크를 구성한다.

블루투스 덕분에 우리가 누릴 수 있는 편리함은 무수히 많다. 걸어다니거나 운전을 하면서 무선 헤드셋을 통해 휴대전화로 통화를 할 수 있게 해주고, 키보드와 마우스를 전선 없이 컴퓨터에 연결할 수 있어서 책상 앞에 앉아 있는 동안 움직임이 보다 유연하고 자유롭도록 해주며, 음악 파일을 아이팟에 쉽게 전송하거나 디지털 카메라에 담긴 사진을 어려움 없이 다운로드할 수 있게 해준다. 블루투스 기술은 또한 사회적 네트워크를 용이하게 해주는 요소이기도 하여, 모르는 사람들이 사정거리 내에서 블루투스가 가능한 모든 다른 장치들을 감지하고 자동적으로 일시적인 네트워크를 형성함으로써 개인 프로필, 메시지, 명함을 주고받을 수 있게 해준다.

그러나 블루투스가 가능케 해주는 네트워크 형성의 용이함은 또한 일부 보안 문제의 원인이 될 수 있다. 블루재킹(Bluejacking)은 시스템에서 발생하는 경고와 유사한 익명의 문자 메시지를 보내는 행위이다. 그것은 해로운 장난은 아니지만 경험이 없는 사용자들을 괴롭게 할 수 있다. 블루스나핑(Bluesnarfing)은 보다 심각한 보안 위협이다. 만일 해커들이 블루투스를 통해 몰래 네트워크를 형성한다면, 그들은 당신의 무선 장치를 통제할 수 있으며 그것을 바이러스를 유포하는 전달 수단으로 사용할 수 있다.

이런 종류의 위협을 예방할 수 있는 조치들에는 장치를 사용하고 있지 않을 때는 블루투스를 꺼놓는 것과 발견 모드를 꺼놓아서 모르는 블루투스 사용자들로부터 당신의 장치를 숨기는 것이 포함된다. 보안 강화를 위해 방화벽과 안티바이러스 소프트웨어를 설치할 수도 있다. 이러한 보안문제들에도 불구하고, 블루투스는 무선 기술 분야의 산업 표준으로서 계속해서 널리 퍼져가고 있으며, 우리의 모든 휴대용 전자 장치들을 연결하는 것을 그 어느 때보다 더 쉽게 만들어주고 있다.

구문 해설

5행 Named in honor of King Harald, Bluetooth technology was developed ...

Bluetooth technology is also a factor ..., **allowing** strangers to exchange personal profiles, ... *by sensing ... range* and automatically *establishing temporary networks.*

▶ allowing 이하는 Bluetooth technology를 부연설명하는 분사구문이다.

▶ sensing ... range와 establishing 이하는 by에 공통으로 걸리는 병렬 구조이다.

22행 However, **the ease with which** Bluetooth creates connections can also be the source ...

▶ However, the ease can also be the source ... + Bluetooth creates connections *with ease.*

31행 ..., Bluetooth continues to reign ..., **making** it easier than ever *to bring together ...*

▶ making 이하는 Bluetooth를 부연설명하는 분사구문이며, it은 to bring together 이하를 진목적어로 하는 가목적어이다.

UNIT 04.
Art

READING 1
p. 20~21

WORD CHECK

1. credo 2. dismiss 3. geometry 4. aesthetic
▶ component: a single part of a larger whole

정답

1. a 2. b 3. b 4. d 5. b 6. unconcerned, minimum, appreciating, cold

해석

미니멀리즘(최소한 표현주의)은 외부의 영향과 보다 심오한 의미에서 벗어나서 존재하는 예술 양식이다. 이것은 사회 문제나 예술가의 감정과는 관계가 없고, 대신 최소한의 요소를 사용함으로써 미를 창조하는 데 초점을 둔다. 미니멀리즘이라는 용어는 1929년에 화가 John Graham의 전시회를 묘사하기 위해 미국에서 처음 사용되었다. 미니멀리즘은 결국 미니멀리즘 운동으로 알려지게 된 것을 설명하기 위해 부활되었던 1960년대에 자주 쓰이는 용어가 되었다.

이 운동은 수학과 기하학에 뿌리를 두면서 정확성에 초점을 두었다. 그 예술 작품은 숨겨진 주제나 의미 없이 단순한 색상의 반복적 패턴을 특징으로 했다. 미니멀리즘 작가들은 복잡한 구성, 심오한 상징, 사회적 주제들이 대상 자체에 대한 감상 경험을 감소시킨다고 생각했다. 미니멀리즘 작가들이 중점을 둔 것은 바로 이러한 감상이었다. 그들의 예술은 자기표현이 아니라 순수한 시각적 결과였다. 그들은 관람객들이 예술을 이해하고자 하는

요구에 의해 산만해지는 것을 원하지 않았다.

미니멀리즘이라는 용어는 이와 유사한 가공하지 않은 의외식으로 만들어진 것이면 어떤 것이든지 그것을 묘사하는 데 사용될 수 있어서, 음악, 디자인, 건축, 문학을 포함한 다양한 범주의 매체에 적용되어 왔다. 음악에서의 미니멀리즘은 반복적인 소리와 일정한 박자를 특징으로 한다. 미니멀리즘 디자인은 기본적인 형태와 깔끔한 선에 의존한다. 미니멀리즘 건축은 또한 빈 공간의 중요성을 강조하고 '적을수록 더 가치가 있다.'는 신조에 동의하면서 극히 적은 장식을 최대한 활용한다. 그리고 문학에서의 미니멀리즘은 단어를 경제적으로 사용하여, 상황의 기초적인 개요만을 묘사하고 평범한 삶을 살아가는 평범한 사람들인 등장 인물들을 특징으로 한다.

놀랄 일도 아니겠지만, 미니멀리즘은 엄청난 비판의 대상이 되어 왔다. 그것은 진정한 예술이라고 보기에는 부족한 것으로 혹은 감정 없고 기계적인 것으로 치부되어 왔다. 미니멀리즘 작가들은 본질적으로 예술계로 하여금 '예술에 의미와 동기가 빠지면 무엇이 남는가?'라는 근본적인 질문에 봉착하도록 했다. 비판론자들은 그것이 "색과 선으로 이루어진 영혼 없는 집합체"라고 말할 것이다. 반대로 미니멀리즘 옹호론자들은 그에 대한 답은 "순수미"라고 주장할 것이다. 그것의 예술적 가치에 대한 개인적인 의견에 관계없이, 미니멀리즘이 후기모더니즘 예술계에 중대한 영향을 미쳤다는 것에는 의심의 여지가 거의 없다.

구문 해설

1행 Minimalism is a style of art [that exists (being) **free of** outside influences ...].

▶ free of 이하는 앞에 being이 생략된 분사구문으로 '~이 없는 상태로'의 의미이다.

8행 Minimalism became ... in the 1960s [**when** it was ... to describe *what* would ...].

▶ [ ]는 the 1960s를 수식하는 때를 나타내는 관계부사절이다.

▶ what은 선행사를 포함하는 관계사로 '~하는 것'의 의미를 지닌다.

13행 **It was** this appreciation **that** minimalists focused on.

▶ It is(was) ~ that ... 강조구문으로 this appreciation을 강조한다.

READING 2   TOEFL
p. 22~23

정답

1. ⓒ 2. ⓓ 3. ⓓ 4. ⓓ 5. The third square
6. ⓐ, ⓒ, ⓕ

해석

옵아트

20세기에는 시각예술에서 혁신적이고 실험적인 분야가 많이 만들어졌다. 그것들 중에 '옵아트,' 즉 '옵티컬 아트'라고 알려지게 된 것이 있었다. 주로 그림에서 발견되는 옵아트는 보는 이가 움직이는 듯한 느낌을 받을 수

있도록 일정한 추상적인 기하학 패턴과 색채대비를 활용한다. 옵아트는 그러한 착시 현상으로 눈속임을 일으키는 것을 통해 보는 행위와 보여지는 것을 인지하는 행위 간의 관계를 탐구한다.

비록 옵아트의 시작이 1920년대까지 거슬러 올라가고, 그 이후로 예술가들이 그것에 대한 실험을 해왔지만, 옵아트는 1960년대 중반이 되어서야 비로소 많은 인정을 받기 시작했다. 1965년 뉴욕에서 〈반응하는 눈〉이라는 국제적인 옵아트 작가들의 전시회는 대중에게 좋은 반응을 얻었다. 예술 비평가들은 감명을 덜 받았지만 1960년대 후반 동안 옵아트의 인기는 꾸준히 증가했다.

옵아트 그림의 두드러진 특징은 이미지가 움직이거나 진동하는 것처럼 보인다는 것이다. 초기의 많은 옵아트 작품들은 주로 흑백으로 이루어졌고, 2차원적인 그림에 깊이감, 형태감, 운동감을 주기 위해 기하학적인 패턴과 선의 반복에 의존했다. 그러한 기법들은 심지어 색깔의 착시 현상을 일으키기도 했다. 칼라로 이루어진 후기 그림들은 보색들이 서로 가까이 놓일 때 생기는 대비 현상의 결과로 보는 이의 눈에 깜박거리거나 진동하는 것 같이 보였다.

비록 옵아트 그림이 3차원 같은 착각을 일으킬 수 있기는 했지만, 그림의 어느 부분이 배경(背景)이고 어느 부분이 전경(前景)인지를 규명하는 것은 종종 어려웠다. 사실 또 다른 유형의 가상의 움직임처럼, 전경과 배경이 계속 자리를 바꾸는 것처럼 보일지도 모른다.

옵아트 운동은 실로 국제적인 운동이다. 이 분야에서 가장 많은 인정을 받은 예술가들 중 두 명은 주로 흑백 작품을 그린 영국의 Bridget Riley와 종종 칼라로 작품을 그린 헝가리의 Victor Vasarely였다. 이 예술가들이 얻은 인정 덕분에 1960년대에 옵아트의 인기가 치솟았고, 그래픽 디자인과 직물 분야에서 옵아트가 등장하기 시작했다. 예를 들어, 여성패션 산업계는 Riley에 의해 유명해진 흑백 스타일을 도입했다. 옵아트에 대한 수요는 1970년대에 접어들면서 줄어들었지만, 예술가들은 오늘날에도 그에 대한 실험을 계속하고 있으며 전시회도 정기적으로 열리고 있다.

구문 해설

[2행] Among them was what came to be known as "op art," or "optical art."
    부사구 / V / S
▶ 부사구가 강조되어 문장 앞으로 나오면서 주어와 동사의 순서가 도치되었다.

[8행] ..., op art did **not** gain much recognition **until** the mid-1960s.
▶ not ~ until ...: …해서야 비로소 ~하다

[16행] Later paintings [that ... color] seemed to flicker ... as a result of the contrast [generated ...].
  S / V
▶ Later paintings [that ... color] seemed to flicker ... as

[18행] ..., **it** was often difficult **to ascertain** *which aspects of the picture were in the background and which occupied the foreground.*
▶ it은 to ascertain 이하를 진주어로 하는 가주어이다.
▶ which aspects ... background와 which ... foreground는 둘 다 간접의문으로 ascertain의 목적어 역할을 한다.

WORD REVIEW TEST

UNIT 01~04   p. 24-25

1. c   2. b   3. d   4. d   5. b   6. c   7. a   8. d
9. attributes   10. inhibits   11. commercials
12. Organic   13. commodity   14. additive
15. flicker   16. calculate   17. c   18. d   19. b
20. b   21. c   22. d   23. resurrect   24. reign
25. ostensible   26. a. 2 b. 3

UNIT 05.
Health

READING 1   p. 26~27

WORD CHECK

1. lifespan   2. restrictive   3. formulate
4. practitioner
▶ consume: to eat or drink a particular thing; to use sth

정답

1. d   2. Both of them encourage a balance between the forces of Yin and Yang.   3. d   4. c   5. b
6. extend, energy, traditional, restrictive

해석

우리들 중 대부분이 '당신의 현재 모습은 당신이 먹은 것의 결과이다.'라는 말을 들어보았을 것이다. 하지만 매크로바이오틱 식이요법(장수식(長壽食))의 창시자에 따르면, 음식은 앞서 언급한 경구가 암시하는 것보다 훨씬 더 많이 우리의 삶에 영향을 미친다. 이 이름이 그리스어 'macro'(긴)와 'bios'(생명)에서 유래하지만, 매크로바이오틱 식이요법이 단순히 수명 연장을 위해 고안된 것은 아니다. 그것은 사람들을 더 행복하게 만들고 그들이 더 넓은 의미의 웰빙을 누리게 하는 것 또한 목표로 한다.

이 식이요법은 일본인 철학자인 George Ohsawa가 창안한 것으로, 그는 매크로바이오틱 식이요법을 체계화하기 위하여 도교의 음양(陰陽) 이원론을 차용했다. 음에 해당하는 음식은 주로 묽고 보다 가벼우며 신선하고 칼륨이 풍부하다. 양에 해당하는 음식은 보다 단단하며 소화시키기는 쉬우면서도 강한 에너지를 제공해 준다. 도교가 실천가들에게 음과 양의 힘 사이에서 삶의 균형을 장려하는 것처럼, 매크로바이오틱 식이요법도 유사한 균형을 찾아가는 방식으로 음식을 먹을 것을 제안한다. 자연의 주기 덕분에 각 계절마다 그리고 심지어는 각 끼니마다 추천되는 음식이 서로 다르다.

선호하는 음식에는 통곡식(껍질을 깎아내지 않은 곡물), 현미, 시리얼, 야채, 과일, 그리고 생선이 포함된다. 매크로바이오틱 식이요법은 실천가들

7

이 가공되었거나 수입된 식품보다는 현지에서 재배된 유기농 식품을 먹도록 권한다. 그것은 심지어 식사를 전기스토브나 전자레인지를 사용하는 현대적 방식보다는 전통적 방식으로 준비하라고 제안한다. 마지막으로 매크로바이오틱 식이요법은 우리에게 식사 준비 과정에서 어떤 재료도 버리지 않도록 가르친다.

매크로바이오틱 식이요법에 대한 연구 결과 낮은 지방 함유량과 높은 섬유질 함유량이 사람들로 하여금 콜레스테롤을 줄여 주고, 심장병의 예방에 효과가 있으며, 암 발병률을 줄여 주고, 체중 조절에 도움을 주며, 면역체계를 강화시켜 주는 이로움이 있다고 한다. 반면에 비판자들은 매크로바이오틱 식이요법이 암과 같은 중환에 걸린 사람들의 치료에 도움을 줄 수 있다는 터무니없는 주장에 대해 납득이 가는 과학적 증거가 없음을 지적한다. 그들은 또한 이 식이요법은 너무 제한적이어서 단백질, 철분, 칼슘, 비타민 B12가 부족하다는 우려의 목소리를 내고 있다.

그러나 매크로바이오틱 식이요법은 우리에게 잘 사는 것과 잘 먹는 것 사이의 중요한 연관성을 상기시켜 준다. 우리의 생활이 보다 분주해지고 스트레스가 많아짐에 따라, 우리가 먹는 것과 그것을 먹는 방법에 대한 전통적인 접근법을 재발견함으로써 우리 모두가 혜택을 볼지도 모른다.

구문 해설

17행 It even **suggests that** meals be prepared by traditional methods *rather than* modern ones ...
▶ suggest that절은 '~해야 한다고 제안하다'의 의미로 that절의 동사 형태는 〈should + 동사원형〉이 되어야 하며 이때의 should는 종종 생략한다.
▶ A rather than B: B라기보다는 오히려 A

25행 ... to the extravagant claims [that the macrobiotic diet ... cure those [**stricken** with ...]].
▶ stricken 이하는 those를 수식하는 과거분사구이다.

26행 They also voice concerns [that the diet is too restrictive], **lacking** protein, ...
▶ lacking 이하는 연속동작을 나타내는 분사구문으로 and it lacks ...로 바꿔 쓸 수 있다.

READING 2
p. 28~29

WORD CHECK

1. ail 2. aural 3. perspiration 4. contraction
▶ involuntary: being automatic and unable to control

정답

1. b 2. b 3. c 4. b-a-d-c 5. d 6. a. heal themselves b. the uses c. how biofeedback therapy works d. different types

해석

의술이 없는 세상에서 살 수 있다면 어떻게 될까? 사람에게 자신의 정신력으로 스스로를 치료할 수 있는 능력이 있다면 어떻게 될까? 공상 과학처럼 들리겠지만, '바이오피드백(생체자기제어)'이라고 일컬어지는 실재의 치료 방법이 신체를 고통스럽게 하는 것을 조절하기 위해 뇌를 사용하도록 사람들을 훈련시키고 있다.

바이오피드백 치료사들은 환자들을 흔히 무의식적인 것으로 여겨지는 혈압 및 뇌 활동에서의 변화와 같은 신체 반응을 조절할 수 있도록 훈련시킨다. 때로는 특정 질병을 치료하는 데 사용되기도 한다. 바이오피드백을 통해 물리치료사는 뇌졸중 환자들이 그들의 근육을 적절히 다시 사용할 수 있도록 훈련시킬 수 있고, 심리학자는 사람들이 느긋한 마음을 갖는 법을 배우도록 도울 수 있으며, 전문의는 환자들에게 고통에 대처하는 방법을 가르칠 수 있다. 또 어떤 때에는 단순히 전반적인 건강을 증진시키기 위해 사용되기도 한다.

바이오피드백은 신체가 스트레스 상황들에 반응하는 방법에 대해 눈에 보이는 결과를 제공함으로써 작용한다. 전형적인 치료 과정 시 측정 장치인 전기 센서가 몸에 부착된다. 이 센서들은 발한 혹은 근육 수축과 같이 스트레스에 대한 신체의 다양한 반응들을 기록할 수 있다. 그런 다음 치료사는 환자에게 시각적 혹은 청각적 연상을 형성시키려고 빛이나 소리 같은 지표를 사용한다. 신체가 특정 방식으로 반응할 때마다 지표가 나타난다. 그러면 환자는 소리나 빛을 조절하기 위해 애쓰도록 지시를 받으며, 그렇게 하는 동안에 신체를 조절하는 법을 배운다.

바이오피드백 치료는 다양한 형태로 여러 가지 질환들을 다룬다. 예를 들어 근전도는 근육의 긴장도를 측정하며, 요통이나 두통 치료에 도움이 될 수 있다. 순환기 장애나 편두통을 앓는 환자들은 피부의 체온을 기록하는 체온 바이오피드백으로 효과를 얻는다. 전기 피부반응훈련은 땀을 측정하며 불안 관련 질환 치료에 도움이 된다. 그리고 뇌파는 도표화되어 불면증 치료에 사용될 수 있으며, 그것은 또한 여러 신경 질환에도 적용될 수 있는 가능성이 있다.

바이오피드백은 의술에 대한 환자의 의존도를 줄이고 신체의 작용 방법에 대한 환자의 의식을 고취시키는 데 효과적인 것으로 보인다. 그것은 또한 의료비를 상당히 줄여줄 가능성도 있다. 그러나 바이오피드백의 진정한 의학적 가치는 여전히 의문스럽다. 과학자들이 이 치료법이 어떻게 작용하는지와 환자들이 자신의 신체 반응을 조절할 수 있는 정확한 수단에 대해 정확하게 설명할 수 있을 때까지 의심의 그림자는 남아있을 것이다.

구문 해설

1행 **What if** we could live in a world without medicine?
▶ What if ~?는 '~하면 어떻게 될까?'의 의미로 What will[would] happen if ~?의 줄임말이다.

17행 **Every time** the body reacts in a certain way, the indicator goes off.
▶ Every time은 접속사처럼 사용되는 명사구로 '~할 때마다'의 의미이다.

29행 Until scientists can accurately explain how ... works (O_1) and the exact means [by which patients can ...] (O_2), **a shadow of doubt** will remain.

▶ Until이 이끄는 부사절에서 동사 explain이 2개의 목적어를 취하고 있는 구조이다.

▶ a shadow of doubt이 문장 전체의 주어이다

UNIT 06.
Language

WORD CHECK

1. geographic   2. reassuring   3. integral
4. superiority
▶ motivation: a specific reason that encourages an action

정답

> 1. a   2. d   3. b   4. Internal code-switching occurs within a single language and external code-switching occurs between two different languages.   5. a. situational code-switching b. external code-switching 6. a. switching codes as a way to communicate b. motivations behind switching codes c. situational vs. metaphorical code-switching d. internal vs. external code-switching e. people's ability to switch codes

해석

언어학에서 개인이 사용하는 화법의 유형은 코드(말하는 방식)라고 불린다. 코드는 언어, 방언, 혹은 심지어 억양이나 말씨가 될 수도 있다. 코드 변환은 개인이 대화 중에 코드를 변경할 때 이루어진다. 때때로 이러한 변환에는 아주 실용적인 이유가 있다. 만일 개인이 하나의 코드로 생각을 표현할 수 없다면 그 사람은 다른 코드로 변환할 것이다.

그러나 또 어떤 때는 코드 변환 이면에 있는 동기들이 보다 복잡한 사회적 의미들을 내포할 수 있다. 그것은 새로운 나라로 이민을 간 사람과 같이 동일한 지리적 또는 사회 경제적 배경을 가진 어떤 사람과의 위안을 주는 유사성을 확인하는 방법이 될 수 있다. 그들은 주간에는 차용어로 말하지만 집에서는 모국어를 섞어 말할 것이다. 코드 변환은 또한 인지된 지적 우월성을 표현하기 위해 사용될 수도 있다. 예를 들어, 교육을 받은 영어 화자들은 그들의 언어 능력을 과시하기 위해 라틴어나 프랑스어 어구를 덧붙일 수 있다.

변환 이면에 있는 동기에 따라 코드 변환은 두 개 유형 중 하나의 범주에 속할 수 있다. 상황적 코드 변환은 그 명칭이 암시하듯이 상황의 변화로 인해 발생한다. 예를 들어 학교에 있는 학생은 운동장에서는 도시 속어가 들어간 말씨를 쓰다가 교실에 들어가서는 표준 영어로 변환할 것이다. 반면에 은유적 코드 변환 이면의 동기는 대화 주제의 변화이다. 노르웨이에서 공식적 업무는 주로 북몰어로 이루어진다. 그러나 보다 일상적인 내용으로 주제가 바뀔 경우 화자는 니노르스크어로 변환할 것이다.

코드 변환의 또 다른 요건은 그것이 내적이냐 외적이냐이다. 내적 코드 변환은 하나의 언어 속에서 어조나 말씨의 변화로 발생한다. 외적 코드 변환은 두 개의 다른 언어 사이에서 발생한다. 인도와 같이 여러 언어를 사용하는 나라에서는 외적 코드 변환이 일상 대화 속에서 무심결에 종종 발생한다. 내적 코드 변환과 외적 코드 변환 모두 상황적 코드 변환이나 은유적 코드 변환 중 하나와 함께 발생할 수 있으며, 그 반대도 마찬가지이다.

모든 사람이 2개 국어를 하는 것은 아니지만, 대부분의 사람들은 한가지 코드 이상을 사용할 수 있는 능력을 가지고 있다. 하나의 코드에서 다른 코드로 언제 변환해야 하는지를 아는 능력은 사람이 자신의 느낌을 효과적으로 표현하기 위해 의존하는 일련의 대화 기술에서 없어서는 안 될 부분이다.

구문 해설

(19행) ... but switch to standard English **when entering** the classroom.
▶ when entering 이하는 때를 나타내는 분사구문으로 when a child enters ...로 바꿔 쓸 수 있다.

(24행) Another qualification of code-switching is **whether it is** internal **or** external.
▶ whether it is A or B는 'A이냐 B이냐'의 의미로 바로 앞에 있는 is의 보어로 쓰였다.

(31행) The ability [to know **when to switch** from ...] is ...
the set of conversational skills [that humans rely on ...].
▶ when to switch는 know의 목적어이며 〈의문사 + to-v〉의 형태로 '언제 ~해야 할 지'의 의미이다.

정답

> 1. ⓑ   2. ⓓ   3. ⓑ   4. ⓓ   5. The second square 6. ⓐ, ⓓ, ⓔ

해석

글로비쉬

세계화는 다른 문화권의 사람들을 서로 접촉하게 하면서 종종 언어 장벽을 드러나게 한다. 어떤 이들은 언어장벽을 해결할 최선의 방법이 전 세계 주민들이 배울 수 있는 전혀 새로운 언어를 만들어 내는 것이라고 생각한다. 그러나 또 어떤 이들은 이것은 비실용적이라고 주장하면서 대신 이미 통용되고 있는 언어의 단순화 혹은 변경을 제안한다. 영어의 간결판인 글로비쉬의 창안은 이러한 생각으로부터 고무된 것이었다.

IBM의 전 부회장인 Jean-Paul Nerriere는 출장 중에 흥미로운 현상을 관찰한 후 글로비쉬를 고안했다. 비(非)영어 원어민인 그는 영어 원어민인 동료들보다 다른 비영어 원어민들과 의사소통을 더 잘했다. 그는 비영어 원어민들이 사실 표준 영어가 아니라 그것을 약간 간결화한 것을 말하는

것이라고 결론지었다. Nerriere는 'global'과 'English' 단어를 합쳐 이 언어 체계를 글로비쉬라고 칭한 후, 공식적인 어휘 목록을 만들어 국제적 의사소통의 효율성 증대를 위한 도구로서 이를 홍보하기 시작했다.

Nerriere의 (글로비쉬) 창안에 있어서의 핵심은 에스페란토나 인터링구아와 같은 완전한 인공 언어들과의 차이점들이다. 글로비쉬는 영어를 기초로 하고 있기 때문에 사람들에게 완전히 새로운 언어 학습을 요구하는 대신 사람들이 이미 가지고 있는 언어적 지식을 토대로 한다. 사실 Nerriere는 글로비쉬가 독자적인 문화나 역사를 나타내지 않기 때문에 전혀 별개의 언어가 아니라고 주장한다. 그것의 목표는 단순히 영어의 기본적이고 가장 필수적인 요소는 취하고 보다 복잡한 측면은 무시하는 것이다. 글로비쉬 사용자는 1,500 단어만을 사용하여 의사소통할 수 있다. 예를 들어 'nephew'라는 단어를 학습하는 대신 화자는 같은 의미를 전달하기 위해 보다 간단한 어구인 '내 남자 형제의 아들'을 사용한다. 또한 글로비쉬는 가장 기본적인 영어 문법 구조만을 사용하며, 발음에 대한 우리의 평가가 완벽성이 아니라 이해에 토대를 두어야 한다고 주장한다.

그러나 모든 언어학 전문가들이 글로비쉬의 유용성에 동의하는 것은 아니다. 가장 흔한 비판 중 하나는 글로비쉬의 어휘 선택에 관한 것이다. 1,500 단어가 어떻게 선정되었는지가 분명하지 않으며, 특정 어휘의 가감은 임의적으로 보인다. 더욱이 글로비쉬의 발음과 문법을 설명하는 Nerriere의 책에는 여러 가지 모순되는 내용이 들어 있어서 이 체계를 배우고자 하는 학습자들 간에 혼란을 야기시키고 있다. 이러한 문제점들을 생각해 볼 때, 글로비쉬가 보다 널리 인정받을 수 있기 전에 더 심도 있게 개발될 필요가 있을 것 같다.

구문 해설

9행 ..., he experienced **more** success in ... speakers **than** his native-speaking associates *did*.

▶ more ~ than ...의 비교급 구문이며, did는 experienced success ... speakers를 가리킨다.

15행 Central to Nerriere's creation are its differences [from such wholly artificial languages ...].
C V S

▶ 〈보어 + 동사 + 주어〉의 도치구문이다.

26행 One of the most frequent criticisms is **with** the selection of Globish's vocabulary.

▶ 전치사 with는 '~에 관하여(대하여)'의 의미를 나타내고 있다.

28행 ..., Nerriere's book [explaining ...] contains various inconsistencies, **causing** confusion ...
S V

▶ causing 이하는 결과를 나타내는 분사구문으로 and it causes ...로 바꿔 쓸 수 있다.

UNIT 07.
Environment

READING 1 p. 34~35

WORD CHECK

1. discard 2. garment 3. synthetic 4. infancy
▶ pesticide: a substance used to kill insects and other pests, especially to protect crops

정답

1. d 2. b 3. d 4. a 5. The amount of waste (that ends up in landfills) is minimized and energy expenditure is reduced (by cutting back on the amount of textiles shipped from abroad). 6. damage, synthetic, pesticides, eco fashion, recycles

해석

최근 몇 년간 환경 보호 문제가 뜨거운 주제로 떠올랐다. 우리는 우리의 행동 방식에 대해 심사숙고하기 시작했고, 그리고는 환경친화적인 대안을 찾아내려고 노력하고 있다. 그러나 지구 보호에 대해 생각할 때, 우리는 대개 우리가 입는 옷에 대해서는 그다지 많이 생각하지 않는다. 그러나 이것을 생각해 보라. 의류 제조업자들이 늘 변화하는 유행 추세에 발맞추기 위한 노력으로 값싼 의류를 신속하게 생산해 오고 있다. 그 옷이 좋아 보일지는 모르겠지만 오래 입도록 만들어지지는 않았다. 그것은 '패스트패션(fast fashion)'이라고 일컬어지는데, 환경에 해를 끼치고 있다.

기업들이 옷을 만들기 위해 선택하는 직물 원료인 나일론이나 폴리에스테르와 같이 값싸고 자연 분해가 되지 않는 합성 물질들이 문제의 커다란 부분을 차지한다. 이 직물들은 대기를 오염시키는 제조 과정을 통해 만들어지고, 버려질 경우 매립지에서 수년간 지하수를 오염시키는 결과를 낳을 수 있다. 합성 직물뿐만 아니라 면처럼 패스트패션에 사용되는 천연 물질도 환경을 훼손시킬 수 있다. 면을 상업적으로 재배할 때는 대부분의 다른 농작물들의 경우보다 살충제가 더 많이 사용되며, 이 직물의 대부분은 나중에 인공 색소로 표백되거나 염색되는데, 이는 지구를 오염시키는 끊임없이 늘어나는 화학물질들의 수를 증가시킨다.

이러한 불건전한 관행에 대한 환경친화적 대응으로 에코패션(eco fashion)이 탄생했다. 해로운 물질로 옷을 제조하는 대신에 에코패션은 삼, 리넨, 유기농법으로 재배한 면과 같은 환경친화적 섬유를 사용한다. 이 섬유들을 식물이나 뿌리로 만든 천연염료로 염색함으로써 기업에서 각 의류를 만드는 데 들어가는 화학물질의 양을 대폭 감소시킬 수 있다. 에코패션은 또한 새로운 옷과 액세서리를 만들기 위해 오래되었거나 버려진 의류 및 기타 재활용 물질을 사용하며, 플라스틱병과 자전거 타이어와 같이 다양하고 어울릴 것 같지 않은 물품들로 최신 유행의 옷을 만든다. 기존 재료를 재활용함으로써 매립지로 전락하는 쓰레기 양이 최소화되고, 해외에서 운송되는 직물의 양을 줄임으로써 에너지 비용이 감소한다.

아직 에코패션 산업이 걸음마 단계에 있지만, 그것은 소비자로서 우리가 내리는 결정의 중요성에 대한 점진적 이해를 나타낸다. 우리가 구매하기로 결정하는 것이 실로 큰 변화를 가져올 수 있다.

구문 해설

`11행` **The textiles** [that companies ... from], **cheap ... polyester**, are a big part of the problem.

▶ The textiles는 cheap ... polyester와 동격 관계에 있다.

`16행` There are more pesticides used in the commercial farming of cotton than **with** most other crops, ..., *which* adds to ...

▶ 전치사 with는 '~에(게)'란 뜻으로 대상을 나타내고 있다.
▶ which는 계속적 용법의 관계대명사로, 앞 문장 전체를 대신하여 and this ...로 바꿔 쓸 수 있다.

`24행` Eco fashion also utilizes ..., **creating** fashionable garments from items [*as* diverse and unlikely *as* plastic bottles and bicycle tires].

▶ creating 이하는 동시동작을 나타내는 분사구문이다.
▶ as ~ as ...: …처럼 ~한

READING 2 　　　　　　　　　　　　　　　 p. 36~37

WORD CHECK

1. incidence　　2. contaminant　　3. in moderation
4. catastrophic
▶ accumulate: to collect, grow, or add up over time

정답

1. b　　2. It's because they play a role in a wide variety of vital life processes, including growth and reproduction.
3. b　　4. c　　5. c　　6. a - ③, b - ①, c - ②, d - ⑤, e - ④

해석

지난 세기 동안 과학기술의 진보는 인간 문명이 번영할 수 있도록 해주었다. 우리는 이전 세대들이 좀처럼 상상할 수 없었던 안락과 편리의 수준에서 살고 있다. 유감스럽게도 이러한 진보의 일부 결과들은 고통스러운 대가를 가져왔는데, 바로 환경 호르몬이다.

우리 몸이 생산해 내는 호르몬은 성장과 생식을 포함한 다양한 필수 생존 과정에서 일익을 담당하기 때문에 우리가 제대로 살아가는 데 없어서는 안 된다. 환경호르몬은 이러한 호르몬의 생성, 분배, 기능에 악영향을 미치는 합성화학물질이며, 심각한 폐해를 가져올 수 있는 파괴 물질이다. 동물들은 이러한 오염물질들에 노출되면서 오랫동안 고통을 당해 왔고, 사람 역시 직접적으로 영향을 받고 있다고 생각하는 데는 근거가 있다.

환경호르몬은 다양한 인공 물질에서 발견된다. 이런 물질들이 환경 속으로 버려질 때 이 해로운 화학물질들은 근처에 사는 어류와 동물들의 지방에 축적된다. 만일 사람이 이렇게 오염된 어류나 동물을 섭취하면 환경호르몬이 사람의 몸속으로 들어갈 수 있다. 이 화학물질들은 또한 그것들을 함유한 제품의 제조 및 처분 과정 중에 공기로도 운반될 수 있어서 호흡을 통해 오염될 가능성이 있다. 그것들은 또한 살충제, 세제 및 기타 물질들과 직접 접촉함으로써 피부를 통해 흡수될 수도 있다.

그렇다면 (환경호르몬에) 노출된 생명체에게는 어떤 일이 일어나는가? 과학자들은 악어에서 독수리까지의 여러 종의 동물에서 선천적 결함, 기형의 생식 기관, 면역력 문제 등을 포함한 심각한 결과들을 관찰했다. 환경호르몬은 성장과 발육에 영향을 미치며, 이런 이유로 인해 태아들이 커다란 위험에 처해 있다는 우려가 있다. 환경호르몬이 젊은 남성들의 생식기와 관련된 암 발병률을 증가시키는 것과 관련이 있다는 증거도 있다.

유기농 음식을 먹고 가정 내 살충제 사용을 피함으로써 환경호르몬에의 노출 위험을 줄일 수 있다. 치즈와 육류 같은 지방질 음식은 적당량을 먹는 것이 가장 좋으며 플라스틱 용기나 식품 포장용 랩에 저장해서는 안된다. 어떤 음식도 플라스틱 형태의 제품에 담아 가열해서는 안 된다. 이러한 조치들은 당신이 오염을 피하도록 하는 데 도움이 될 수는 있겠지만 우리 사회가 직면한 문제를 해결하지는 못할 것이다. 과학과 기술은 스스로가 만든 곤란한 상황을 해결하기 위해 효과적인 방법을 마련해야 한다.

구문 해설

`8행` Endocrine disruptors are synthetic chemicals [that ...], a disruption [that ...].

▶ a disruption 이하는 앞 문장에 대한 부연 설명이다.

`16행` These chemicals can also become ..., **leading to** the possibility of contamination ...

▶ leading to 이하는 결과를 나타내는 분사구문이다.

`20행` Scientists have observed severe consequences [in a variety ...], [including birth defects ...].

▶ 2개의 [ ]는 각각 전치사구, 현재분사구로서 severe consequences를 수식하고 있다.

UNIT 08.
Archaeology

READING 1 　　　　　　　　　　　　　　　 p. 38~39

WORD CHECK

1. indigenous　　2. depression　　3. terrace
4. microclimate
▶ porous: having a number of holes that fluid can pass through

정답

해석

페루에 있는 예전 잉카의 수도인 쿠스코에서 북서쪽으로 약 50km, 해발 약 3,500m 위에 놀랍고 신비스러운 잉카 문명의 유적이 연속해서 존재한다. 모라이라고 불리는 이 고고학적 유적지는 여러 개의 거대하고, 그릇처럼 움푹 패인 부분들로 이루어져 있는데, 각각 연속적인 원형 계단식 논을 형성하고 있다. 비록 이 움푹 패인 곳이 어떤 목적을 위한 것이었는지는 불확실하지만, 대부분의 고고학자들은 농업 연구를 시행하기 위해 사용되었다는 데에 의견을 일치하고 있다.

모라이가 가지고 있는 여러 놀라운 특징들이 이곳을 농업 연구를 행하기 위한 이상적인 장소로 만들었을 것이다. 첫째로, 움푹 패인 곳의 가장 윗부분에서 가장 낮은 지점까지 15도 만큼의 상당한 온도 차가 존재한다. 그 결과, 오늘날 온실과 흡사하게 각 움푹 패인 곳은, 특정 기후를 가지고 있는 좁은 지역인 여러 미기후 지역을 포함하게 된다. 이보다 더 믿기 힘든것은, 이러한 다른 온도 차가 해안가 농지에서부터 고지대 계단식 논에 이르는 주변 지역의 자연 기후와 일치한다는 것이다. 이것은 잉카 사람들이 상이한 온도 조건이 농작물에 어떤 영향을 끼치는지에 대하여 한 곳에서 모두 연구할 수 있도록 만들었을 것이다. 심지어 꽃가루 연구에서도 잉카 제국의 여러 지역에서 온 흙이 모라이로 유입되었음을 보여주고 있다. 이는 다른 지역의 재배 조건을 거의 완벽하게 다시 만드는 것을 가능케 했었을 것이다.

모라이의 두 번째 놀라운 특징은 배수 장치이다. 움푹 패인 곳의 그릇 형태의 모양 때문에 폭우 기간에 움푹 패인 곳의 낮은 부분들은 쉽게 물로 가득 찰 것 같아 보인다. 하지만 폭우 속에서도 그 구조물은 절대 범람하지 않는다. 그 움푹 패인 곳에서 어떻게 물이 빠지는지는 미스터리로 남아있지만, 바닥에 있는 지하 수로가 아마 물을 뺀다는 설이 있다. 또 다른 이론은 움푹 패인 곳이 아주 투과성이 높은 천연 암석 위에 위치해 있어 물이 끊임없이 여과될 수 있다고 제시하고 있다.

놀랍게도 수백 가지 종류의 다양한 옥수수와 수천 가지의 다양한 감자를 포함한 세계 식용 작물의 약 60퍼센트가 안데스 산맥에서 비롯되었다. 이것은 지역 토착민들이 그 지역의 각기 다른 기후에 잘 맞는 작물을 재배하는 데 얼마나 능숙했는지를 보여준다. 비록 모라이가 왜 만들어졌는지 결코 확실히 알 수는 없겠지만, 그 장소가 잉카 제국의 다양한 토지를 최대한 활용하기 위한 방법을 배우기 위해 사용됐을 가능성은 아주 높다.

구문 해설

7행　Although the purpose [that these depressions served] is uncertain, most archaeologists agree [that they were used to carry out agricultural research].

▶ 첫 번째 [ ]는 the purpose를 수식하는 목적격 관계대명사절이다.

▶ 두 번째 [ ]는 명사절로 agree의 목적어로 쓰였다.

15행　This would have **allowed** the Inca **to study** [*how* different climatic conditions affected crops all in one place].

▶ 'allow + 목적어 + to부정사' 구문으로 allow는 목적격보어로 to 부정사를 취한다. '~가 …하는 것을 가능하게 하다'라는 의미이다.

▶ how 이하는 study의 목적어 역할을 하는 간접의문문으로 '~하는 방법'으로 해석된다.

22행　How the depressions drain remains a mystery, **but it has been suggested** that …

▶ 'have[has] been p.p' 구문으로 현재완료수동태이다.

READING 2　TOEFL　p. 40~41

정답

해석

이집트 상형문자의 해독

1799년에 한때 Rosetta라고 알려졌던 이집트 마을 근처에 요새를 재건하던 프랑스 군대가 흥미로운 물체를 발견했다. '로제타석(Rosetta Stone)'이라고 이름 지어진 이것은 고대 이집트의 상형문자 해독의 열쇠임이 드러났다.

로제타석은 이집트의 통치자 Ptolemy V Epiphanes의 대관식 1주년이던 기원전 196년에 만들어졌다. 비문은 이집트 성직자들이 Ptolemy를 지지한다는 내용을 말하고 있고 그의 통치하에 국가가 입은 혜택의 내용을 나열하고 있다. 그것은 또한 성직자들이 그 통치자에게 수여한 여러가지 영예와 특권을 언급하고 있다. 학자들은 그 돌이 모든 이집트인들 사이에서 Ptolemy에 대한 충성을 강화하기 위해 계획된 그런 여러 공식적 행위 중 하나였다고 믿는다.

세로 약 112cm, 가로 약 75cm 크기인 매끄럽고 짙은 회색의 석판인 로제타석에는 정확하게 똑같은 내용의 비문이 세 개의 서로 다른 문자로 기록되어 있다. 첫째는 주로 당시의 중요한 종교 문서에 사용되었던 고대 활자인 이집트 상형문자이다. 둘째는 Ptolemy의 통치 기간 동안 평민들이 사용한 초서체 유형의 활자인 데모틱 문자이다. 마지막 활자는 그리스어인데, 이는 이 시대의 이집트 관리 수뇌들과 실제로 Ptolemy 자신도, 그리스 출신이었기 때문이다.

이집트학에 있어서 로제타석의 중요성은 엄청나다. 거의 모든 고대 이집트 문서는 상형문자로 쓰였는데 이 글자 체계에 대한 지식은 그것이 쓰이지 않게 된 서기 400년경에 사라졌다. 이런 이유로 1800년 이전의 이집트학자들은 그런 문서에 담긴 정보를 알아낼 방법이 없었다. 로제타석의 중요성은 그것이 상형문자와 그리스어 간의 비교점을 제공해 주어 학자들이 상형문자 해독의 열쇠로 그리스어 비문을 사용할 수 있게 하였다는 점이다.

로제타석 연구 과정 중에 프랑스의 이집트학자 Jean-François Champollion은 중대한 발견을 했다. 이전에는 상형문자가 말하기 위해서가 아니라 오로지 읽혀지기 위한 것이라고 여겨졌었다. 다시 말해, 이집트 학자들은 상형문자가 특정 구어의 음과 대응하지 않는다고 생각했다. 이와 반대되는 Champollion의 결론은 획기적인 전환이 되어 연구원들로 하여금 수많은 상형문자 문서를 해독하고 고대 이집트 문명에 대해 아주 귀중한 정보를 얻을 수 있게 하였다. 그와 그 외 많은 이들의 작업 덕분에, 1799년에 프랑스 군대에 의한 이 우연한 발견이 우리가 현재 고대 이집트에 대해 알고 있는 많은 것들을 얻는 계기가 되었다.

구문 해설

[1행] In 1799, French troops [reconstructing ... an Egyptian town [once known as Rosetta]] discovered ...
S

V

▶ reconstructing ... Rosetta는 현재분사구로서 French troops를 수식하고, once ... Rosetta는 과거분사구로서 an Egyptian town을 수식한다.

[2행] (Being) **Named** the "Rosetta Stone," it turned out to be *the key to deciphering* ...

▶ Named ... Stone은 앞에 Being이 생략된 분사구문으로 주어인 it에 대한 부연설명이다.

▶ the key to + 명사상당어구: ~의 열쇠

[18행] The significance of the Rosetta Stone was **that** it provided ..., *allowing* scholars to use ...

▶ that절이 문장의 보어 역할을 하고 있다.

▶ allowing 이하는 결과를 나타내는 분사구문으로 and it allowed ...로 바꿔 쓸 수 있다.

WORD REVIEW TEST

p. 42-43

1. c   2. b   3. d   4. c   5. d   6. a   7. b
8. discard   9. condensed   10. perspiration
11. privileges   12. Conducting   13. expenditure
14. superiority   15. stunning   16. inconsistency
17. c   18. a   19. d   20. b   21. a   22. b
23. remarkable   24. indigenous   25. garment
26. a. 3 b. 2

UNIT 09.
Film

READING 1
p. 44~45

WORD CHECK

1. refinement   2. subtle   3. project   4. portray
▶ dazzling: being of intensely impressive or beautiful quality

정답

1. c   2. It's because it records (not only general body movements but also) subtle facial expressions.   3. b - a - d - c   4. b   5. d   6. a - ②, b - ⑤, c - ①, d - ④, e - ③

해석

당신은 그들이 영화 속 화면에서 살아나는 것을 보았다. 그들은 실제로 살아 있지는 않지만 그들의 움직임은 실제처럼 보이고 그들의 얼굴은 감정을 드러낸다. 그렇다면 무엇이 〈폴라 익스프레스〉와 〈아바타〉와 같은 영화 속에 나오는 등장인물들을 그렇게 살아 있는 것처럼 보이게 하는 걸까? 그것은 그것들이 모두 연기와 '퍼포먼스 캡처'라고 불리는 디지털 효과의 결합으로 만들어졌기 때문이다.

퍼포먼스 캡처는 모션 캡처라고 불리는 특수 효과 기술의 진보된 형태이다. 모션 캡처는 애니메이션 영화와 비디오게임에서 가상 인물이 매우 사실적으로 움직이게 해주는 것이다. 그것은 실제 인물의 움직임들을 포착해서 그것들을 컴퓨터로 만들어 낸 등장인물에 적용함으로써 창조된다. 그러나 퍼포먼스 캡처는 이것을 한 단계 더 진보시켜 일반적인 신체의 움직임뿐만 아니라 미세한 얼굴 표정까지도 포착해 낸다.

퍼포먼스 캡처로 하나의 등장인물이 살아나게 하기 위해, 우선 배우의 얼굴과 신체를 작은 감지기들로 뒤덮는다. 그런 다음 배우가 검정색 특수 상자 안으로 들어가서 연기를 하는 동안 적외선 카메라는 3차원의 효과가 나도록 네 군데 각도에서 그 움직임을 기록한다. 이렇게 기록한 것들을 이용해 소프트웨어가 배우의 연기를 디지털화하여 컴퓨터로 만들어 낸 등장인물들에게 전이시킨다. 그런 다음 이 등장인물들이 가상의 소품과 가상의의상이 완비된 아주 섬세한 가상 세트에 투영되면서 실제와 같은 환상이 이루어진다.

퍼포먼스 캡처는 영화 제작자에게 시간이 많이 걸리는 종래의 애니메이션 방법에 대해 보다 신속한 대안을 제공하며, 보다 자연스러운 움직임과 얼굴 표정을 만들어 주기도 한다. 그리고 실제 배우를 사용하는 장면들과 비교해볼 때, 편집 과정이 보다 통제 가능하다. 만일 장면에서 뭔가가 잘못되었을 경우, 그것을 다시 찍을 필요가 없다. 그냥 컴퓨터로 수정하면 그만이다. 또한 배우 입장에서도 퍼포먼스 캡처는 과거에 라텍스 마스크나 특수 효과로 가려졌을 복잡한 얼굴 표정을 사용하면서 연기를 할 수 있게 하기 때문에 이득이 된다. 그것은 심지어 Tom Hanks가 산타클로스와 어린 소년을 포함한 5명의 다른 등장인물들을 연기한 〈폴라 익스프레스〉에서와 같이 한 사람의 배우가 다수의 역할을 할 수 있게 한다.

퍼포먼스 캡처는 영화 제작자들에게 배우의 능력과 특수 효과 전문가들의 역량 사이에서 작업 균형을 이루게 하면서 두 분야에서 최선의 능력을 발휘하게 한다. 그 결과 수백만 관객들은 마술과 같은 눈부신 영화 장면들을 접하게 된다.

구문 해설

[17행] The characters are ... a highly detailed virtual set, [(which is) **complete** ...], and the illusion of reality ...

[25행] ... because it lets him or her act **using** complex facial expressions [that in the past *would have been lost* ...].

▶ using 이하는 동시동작을 나타내는 분사구문이다.

▶ would have been lost 이하는 가정법 과거 완료의 귀결절을 나타내는 것으로 볼 수 있으며 'if it had been in the past, they would have been lost ...'의 의미이다.

[29행] Performance capture brings filmmakers ..., **affording** a workable balance ...

▶ affording 이하는 동시동작을 나타내는 분사구문이다.

READING 2
p. 46~47

WORD CHECK

1. immerse   2. manifest   3. pull off   4. persona

▶ demanding: difficult or challenging

정답

1. d   2. c   3. c   4. a   5. d   6. technique, performances, motivations, recreate, problems

해석

유명 배우인 Marlon Brando는 몇 편의 할리우드 최고 흥행작에서의 명연기로 이름이 알려져 있다. Marilyn Monroe와 James Dean은 둘 다 사망 이후에조차 그들이 만들어 낸 영화 속 인물들로 칭송되고 있는 영화계의 전설들이다. 그리고 이들 셋은 모두 '메소드 연기'로 알려진 기법을 사용하여 영화에 마술을 부렸다.

메소드 배우들은 자신이 배역을 맡은 등장인물들의 행동 이면에 있는 심리적 동기를 분석하고 이해함으로써 사실적인 연기를 하려고 노력한다. 이 기법은 20세기 전환기 즈음에 러시아의 Konstantin Stanislavski에 의해 처음 개발되었다. 그리고 그것은 미국의 감독이자 프로듀서이고 연기 교사였던 Lee Strasberg에 의해 인기를 얻게 된 1950년대에 미국에서 다시 부활되었다.

메소드 연기는 대본 밖에서는 존재하지 않는 사람들에 대해 복잡한 감정을 부여할 것을 요구하기 때문에 그것을 사용하는 배우들에게 많은 부담을 준다. 배우들은 왜 등장인물들이 그러한 방법으로 행동하고 느끼는지를 더 잘 이해하기 위해 가상의 경험과 사건을 이용하면서 그들이 연기하고 있는 등장인물의 전체적인 이력을 세워 놓는다. 그런 다음 배우들은 유사한

감정을 만들어 주는 경험에 대한 자신의 개인적인 기억들을 깊이 더듬어 보면서 이러한 감정들을 자신들 속에서 재창조하려고 노력한다. 만일 메소드 연기가 제대로 되면 배우들은 완전히 몰입하여, 그 결과 영화 관객 들이 쉽게 잊지 못할 아주 사실적인 연기를 이끌어 낼 수 있게 된다.

그러나 메소드 연기는 많은 훈련을 필요로 하며 연기자에게 정신적, 신체적 손해를 많이 끼칠 수 있다. 어떤 배우들은 너무 깊이 몰입한 나머지 위험에 처하기도 한다. 이는 실험적 마약 복용과 같은 것으로 나타났었는데, River Phoenix의 경우 이것이 마약 과다 복용으로 인한 사망을 초래했다. 보다 일반적이고 덜 심각한 부정적인 결과는 바로 서툰 연기이다. 제대로 구현되지 못한 메소드 연기는 영화 역사에 있어 일부 가장 볼품없는 연기를 초래했다.

메소드 연기의 힘든 요구 조건들을 훌륭히 해내지 못하는 재능 없는 연기자들도 있지만, Al Pacino, Robert De Niro, 그리고 Dustin Hoffman 등 자신의 역할에 그것을 성공적으로 적용시킨 몇몇 현대 할리우드 배우들이 있다. 그들의 연기력은 연기에 대한 이 독특한 접근으로부터 빼어난 결과를 얻어낼 수 있는 가능성이 있음을 증명한다.

구문 해설

[13행] Method acting places ..., **requiring** them to create complex emotions for people [that don't ...].

▶ requiring 이하는 이유를 나타내는 분사구문으로 as it requires ...로 바꿔 쓸 수 있다.

[15행] ..., **using** ... in order to better understand [*why* the characters ... feel the way [they do]].

▶ using 이하는 동시동작을 나타내는 분사구문으로 '~하면서'의 의미이다.

▶ why 이하는 understand의 목적어 역할을 하는 간접의문문으로 '왜 ~하는지'로 해석된다.

[23행] This has manifested itself in ... experimental drug use, [**which** ... actually led to death ...].

▶ [ ]는 선행사 experimental drug use를 부연 설명하는 계속적 용법의 관계대명사절로, 이때의 which는 and it으로 바꿔 쓸 수 있다.

UNIT 10.
Psychology

READING 1
p. 48~49

WORD CHECK

1. temper   2. conscience   3. incorporate   4. referee

▶ fulfillment: the situation when all needs and requirements have been met

해석

혹자가 한번은 정신에 대한 Sigmund Freud의 견해를 묘사하면서 인간의 인성은 '근본적으로 전쟁터, 즉 예의바른 미혼 여성과 쾌락을 추구하는 원숭이가 상당히 신경질적인 은행 직원이 심판을 보는 가운데 끊임없이 사투를 벌이는 어두운 지하실'이라고 말한 적이 있다. 이 기이한 등장인물들이 성격과 어떤 관계가 있는지를 이해하기 위해서는 Freud가 생각한 정신의 구조를 분석해야 한다.

정신을 빙산이라고 생각해 보라. 눈에 보이는 빙산의 꼭대기 부분은 우리가 인식하고 있는 정신의 작은 영역인 의식에 견주어진다. 정신의 대부분을 차지하는 영역은 무의식으로서, 물속에 잠긴 거대한 빙산처럼 우리의 의식 밑에 깔려 있다. Freud가 정신을 이 두 영역으로 나눈 것은 추후에 보다 포괄적인 개념인 구조이론으로 통합되었는데, 이 이론은 정신을 이드, 초자아, 자아라는 세 가지 영역으로 나눔으로써 정신의 복잡함을 보다 정확히 묘사하려 했다.

Freud의 이론에 따르면, 이드는 무의식 속에 완전히 묻혀 있는 정신의 한 영역이다. 사람으로 하여금 쾌락을 추구하고 고통을 회피하게 하는 본능적인 충동은 이곳에서 기인한다. 인간 정신의 또 다른 영역은 초자아로 불린다. 부분적으로 의식 영역을 차지하고 있는 초자아는 도덕적 양심역할을 하여, 그것이 정하는 선악의 기준으로 이드의 욕구를 조절한다. 마지막으로 Freud의 세 번째 정신 영역인 자아는 주로 의식적 사고 수준에서 활동한다. 외부 현실에 신경을 쓰는 자아는 타인의 욕구를 의식하며 이드와 초자아의 습성이 조절되어야 한다는 것을 인식하고 있다.

이 세 가지 정신 영역의 상호 작용이 아주 필수적이라는 사실은 분명한데 이것들이 서로 맞물려 세상과 원활히 상호 작용하는 인격을 형성하기 때문이다. 이드가 지나치게 지배하게 되면 사람이 오직 자신의 욕구 충족에만 신경을 쓰고 타인에게 전혀 무관심할 것이다. 초자아가 지배하면 사람이 아주 편협해져서 타인의 도덕적 결점을 수용하는 능력 부족으로 외로운 삶을 영위할 것이다. 결국 균형 잡힌 인격에는 자아가 필수불가결인데, 이것이 없으면 사람이 이드와 초자아의 서로 다른 욕구를 조화롭게 할 수 없을 것이기 때문이다.

구문 해설

3행 ... "basically a battlefield ... a dark cellar [in which ... are forever engaged in mortal combat, the struggle [being refereed by ...]]."

▶ 바깥 [ ]는 a dark cellar를 수식하는 〈전치사 + 관계대명사절〉로 in which를 관계부사 where로 바꿔 쓸 수 있다.

13행 ... was later incorporated into a ... conception, the structural theory, [which attempted ...].

▶ which 이하는 the structural theory를 부연 설명하는 주격관계대명사절이다.

25행 It is obvious that the interplay ... essential, for they mesh together to form a personality [that interacts ...].

▶ It은 가주어이고, that ... essential이 진주어이다.

▶ to form 이하는 결과의 to부정사구로 앞에서부터 순차적으로 해석하는 게 자연스럽다.

해석

인지 부조화

사람의 세계관은 수많은 인지, 즉 사실, 믿음, 가치관, 감정 등의 정보 조각으로 이루어져 있다. 전 생애에 걸쳐 사람은 새로운 정보에 직면할 때 계속해서 새로운 인지를 하게 된다. 그 과정에서 새로운 인지가 이전에 지니고 있던 인지와 마찰을 일으키면 '인지 부조화'라는 결과를 가져온다.

인지 부조화는 불안감을 조성한다. 예를 들어, 한 남자가 비싼 자동차는 연비가 좋다고 생각하여 비싼 자동차를 산다. 그 후 그는 연비가 훨씬 좋은 좀 더 저렴한 자동차에 대한 광고를 본다. 자신이 처음 지니고 있던 인지가 새로운 인지와 충돌하기 때문에 남자는 당연히 속이 상한다. 사람에게는 원래 인지 부조화를 회피하고 싶은 욕구가 있고, 이것은 여러 가지 방법으로 해결될 수 있다. 앞의 예에서 남자는 그저 광고를 무시하는 쪽을 택할 수 있다. 그런 다음 그 후로 그 TV 광고를 보지 않으려고 할지도 모른다. 인지 부조화를 제거하는 또 하나의 방법은 그 상황에 새로운 인지를 도입하는 것이다. 남자는 자신이 소유하고 있는 자동차의 다른 긍정적인 특징들을 강조하기 시작하여 연비와 가격의 중요도를 축소시킬 수 있다. 그리고 만일 인지 부조화 정도가 극도로 심해지면 남자는 자신의 자동차를 그 저가의 자동차로 바꿀지도 모른다.

인지 부조화의 영향력을 경시하기 쉬운데, 이것은 여러 실험에서 입증되어 왔다. 1950년대에 연구원 Leon Festinger는 교주로부터 외계인들이 특정 날짜에 지구를 파괴할 것이라는 말을 들은 어느 신흥 종교 신자들을 연구했다. 그 날이 왔고 아무 일도 일어나지 않은 이후 이 종교 신자들은 자신들의 교주에 대한 믿음이 훨씬 더 커졌다. Festinger의 설명에 의하면 신자들은 자신들이 속았다는 인지를 받아들이기보다는 외계인들이 자신들의 종교를 구하기 위해 지구를 그대로 둔 것이라는 교주의 새로운 메시지를 믿는 쪽을 택한 것이라고 한다.

확실히 인지 부조화는 사람들로 하여금 비이성적인 방법으로 행동하게끔 할 수 있다. 그러나 그것은 또한 분쟁 해결과 같이 긍정적으로 사용될 가능성도 있다. 인지 부조화는 이전에 지니고 있던 믿음과 가치관에 제동을 걸어 사람들로 하여금 그것들을 바꾸게 할 수 있다. 전쟁에서 각 진영은 상대를 비인간적이나 심지어 사악하다고 여길 수 있다. 이러한 인지에 맞설 수 있는 한 가지 방법으로 적군의 가정생활에 대해 얘기하거나 그 예를 들어 주며 두 진영의 유사점을 강조하는 것이 될지도 모른다. 각 진영에게 상대의 인간적인 측면을 보여 줌으로써 처음 가졌던 고정관념이 인지 부조화의 영향에 도전을 받게 되어 극복될 수도 있는 것이다.

구문 해설

15행 It is easy **to discount** the power of cognitive dissonance, but *it* has been ...
▶ 첫 번째 It은 to discount ... dissonance를 진주어로 하는 가주어이고, 두 번째 it은 the power of cognitive dissonance를 가리키는 대명사이다.

16행 ... studied the members of a cult [who **had been told by** their leader [*that* aliens would ...]].
▶ 바깥 [ ]는 the members of a cult를 수식하는 주격 관계대명사절이다.
▶ A is told by B that ~: A가 B에게서 ~이라는 말을 듣다
▶ that 이하는 had been told의 목적어 역할을 한다.

25행 A tactic ... might be ┌ to discuss
├ or (to) give examples ...
└ and (to) emphasize similarities ...

UNIT 11.
Social Issues

READING 1
p. 52~53

WORD CHECK

1. rigor   2. devoid of   3. bleak   4. succeeding
▶ adolescence: the period between childhood and adulthood

정답

1. b   2. a   3. c   4. The world may be faced with a generation devoid of economic and political leaders.
5. a   6. adulthood, education, economy, carefree

해석

단어 '트윅스터(twixter)'는 전 세계적으로 급속히 늘어나고 있는 집단인 청소년기와 성인기 사이 어딘가에 존재하는 새로운 사회 집단을 칭하기 위해 만들어졌다. 그것은 'between'과 같은 의미를 지니는 단어 'betwixt'에서 유래했다.

트윅스터는 더 이상 청소년이 아니면서 아직 전형적인 어른처럼 행동하지 않고 있는 '20대'이다. 그들은 돈을 모으는 것보다 삶을 즐기는 것에 더 관심이 많고, 직장으로부터 급여 외에 훨씬 더 많은 것을 기대하기 때문에 직장을 자주 바꾼다. 그들 중 많은 이들은 재정적 지원을 받기 위해 부모에게 의지하면서 여전히 본가에 산다. 적정 수입이 없이 트윅스터들은 우리 사회가 성인기를 규정하는 두 가지 기초 요소인 결혼과 집을 추구할 마음이 없다.

트윅스터식 생활양식에 대해 책임이 있는 것으로 꼽을 수 있는 한 가지 원인은 없다. 대신 여러 요인들이 결합되어 있는 것 같다. 늘어나는 실업률과 느린 경제 성장은 일자리를 구하는 것을 그 어느 때보다도 힘들게 하고 있다. 대학 경험이 학생들에게 실제 직업에 대한 대비를 적절히 해주지 못하고 있다는 말도 나오고 있다. 게다가 계속 오르는 고등 교육비는 많은 트윅스터들이 과중한 부채 부담을 안고 졸업하여 경제적 독립을 이루는 데 걸리는 시간이 늘어남을 의미한다.

트윅스터들의 수가 계속 증가함에 따라 그들은 사회에 심각한 부담으로 드러나기 시작하고 있다. 일부 경제학자들은 그들을 이후 세대들이 동일한 경제적 악순환에 빠지게 되는 미래에 대한 어두운 징조로 본다. 만일 트윅스터들이 자신의 성인기를 제대로 받아들이지 못한다면, 세상은 경제 및 정치 지도자가 없는 세대를 맞이하게 될지도 모른다.

트윅스터를 보는 시각들은 다르다. 일부 사회학자 및 심리학자들은 긍정적인 측면에 초점을 둔다. 그들은 트윅스터들이 그저 풍족한 사회가 제공하는 혜택들을 이용하고 있는 것일 뿐이라고 생각한다. 그들은 성인기의 어려움을 준비하기 위해 상대적으로 걱정이 없는 청소년기를 연장하면서 한 가지 진로나 생활양식에 전념하기 전에 여러 가지 경우를 경험하고 있다는 것이다. 그러나 어떤 이들은 그들을 스스로 생존하는 데 필요한 도구를 갖추고 있지 못한 실패한 어른과 같이 보다 부정적인 시각으로 바라본다. 그래서 어떤 이들에게는 트윅스터가 이상주의 세대를 대표하는 반면, 어떤 이들에게는 게으름에서 벗어나지 못한 사람들의 불필요한 사회 집단에 불과하다.

구문 해설

1행 ... was coined to refer to a new social group [that exists ...], a group [that is ...].
▶ 2개의 [ ]는 각각 a new social group과 a group을 수식하는 주격 관계대명사절이다.

5행 They're more concerned ..., **changing** jobs often *as* they expect a lot more ...
▶ changing 이하는 동시동작을 나타내는 분사구문이다.
▶ as는 이유의 접속사로 쓰였으며 '~이기 때문에'의 의미이다.

29행 ..., while for others they are **nothing more than** an unwanted social group of people [who ...].
▶ nothing more than: ~에 지나지 않는 (= only)

READING 2
p. 54~55

WORD CHECK

1. alienate   2. meticulously   3. perpetrate   4. stunt
▶ vicious: being of extremely hurtful and upsetting quality

정답

1. d 2. a 3. a 4. c 5. a. spreading fear b. various factors c. gain public attention d. economic effects

해석

　　테러는 공포를 불러일으켜 사회적 혹은 정치적 변화를 일으키고자 한다. 이러한 공포는 주로 현 상태의 지배력과 영향력을 약화시키기 위해 사용된다. 비록 테러에 대한 현대적 개념이 19세기 후반 이래로 존재해오긴 했지만, 2001년 미국의 9·11 테러 공격의 엄청난 규모는 전 세계에 공포의 충격을 안겨 주었다.

　　테러는 역사와 같이 공존해 왔다. 종교적 박해, 정치적 억압, 경제적 착취, 문화적 지배, 인종 차별, 혹은 이런 것들이 결합된 형태의 이유로 인해 소외되어 왔던 단체들이 주로 테러를 저질렀다. 어떤 경우에는 자신의 신앙이 유일한 진짜 종교라고 믿는 극단주의자들이 테러에 가담해 왔다. 때때로 테러 행위는 자신들의 권리가 묵인되거나 자신들에게 아무런 법적 출구가 없다고 생각하는 사람들에 의해 자행된다. 현대적 테러는 흔히 우리가 전 세계적으로 보게 되는 만연한 부의 불균형에 의해 유발된다.

　　9·11 테러 공격은 극단적이었으나 현대적 테러가 점점 더 치명적으로 되어감을 보여 주는 중요한 예에 해당한다. 테러는 임의대로 이루어지는 폭력 행위들로 이루어지지 않는다. 각각의 공격은 특정 목적을 이루기 위한 수단으로 치밀하게 계획되어진다. 대상들은 세심하게 선정되는데, 흔히 무고한 시민들의 목숨을 희생시킴으로써 공포를 극대화할 수 있도록 선정된다. 이러한 노력들은 모두 공포를 불러일으키고 매체의 관심을 끌기 위해서 아주 정확하게 조율된다. 그리고 테러 단체들은 오늘날의 세계화된 사회에서 국제적인 관심을 얻으려고 하기 때문에 이 목적을 달성하기 위해 점점 공격을 확대해 나가고 있다.

　　비록 테러의 가장 명백한 결과가 인명의 피해이기는 하지만 그것은 또한 경제적 타격을 입힐 가능성도 있다. 재산 손실액 및 공격 이후 잇따르는 보험 청구액의 총계는 종종 엄청난 액수에 이른다. 금융업계는 공포에 의해 혼란에 빠져, 때로는 주식 시장의 붕괴까지 초래된다. 이런 이유로 테러는 경제 성장을 저해하거나 혹은 심지어 국가 경제를 무너뜨릴 가능성도 있다. 그리고 테러가 국제적인 규모로 커짐에 따라 영향을 받는 것도 국제 경제가 되고 있다.

　　현대적 테러가 예방되려면 그 원인들이 이해되어야 한다. 테러 단체의 저변 동기가 무엇이든지 간에 무고한 시민들에게 영향을 미치는 악의적인 행위에 대해서는 변명의 여지가 없다.

구문 해설

9행　Groups [that have been alienated because of ...] usually **perpetrate** it.
　▶ 전체 문장의 동사는 perpetrate이다.

13행　Sometimes, terrorist acts are committed by people [who feel **that** ... or **that** ...].
　▶ 2개의 that절은 feel의 목적절로 쓰였다.

20행　These efforts are ..., ┌ creating fear
　　　　　　　　　　　　　└ and
　all in the interest of　└ gaining media attention.

29행　..., **it is** the global economy **that** is affected.
　▶ it is ~ that ... 강조구문으로 주어 the global economy 를 강조하고 있다.

UNIT 12.
Education

READING 1　　　　　　　　　　　　p. 56~57

WORD CHECK

1. demeanor　2. friction　3. regularity
4. predisposition
▶ adapt: to grow and change in order to meet changing circumstances or needs

정답

1. d　2. b　3. c　4. to better understand their children both as individuals and members of the family unit　5. a　6. a. factors involved in shaping personalities b. (nine) temperament traits that characterize young children c. three categories of children's personalities d. effects of a child's temperament on family life

해석

　　생물학적 요인 및 환경적 요인 둘 다 인격 형성에 관련이 있다고 오랫동안 여겨져 왔다. 유전적으로 결정되는 특징들은 개인의 '기질'이라고 일컬어진다.

　　연구자들은 초기 발달 단계에 있는 어린 아동들을 특징짓는 아홉 가지 기질적 특징들을 밝혀냈다. 이 특징들은 절대적인 것이라기보다는 아동에 따라 각각의 특징을 더 많이 혹은 더 적게 보인다고 할 수 있다. 구체적으로 말하자면 각 행동은 신체 에너지, 생리적 기능의 규칙성, 낯선 환경이나 새로운 사람들에 대한 초기 반응, 장기적 변화에의 순응성, 어떤 상황에 대한 아동의 반응 강도, 외부 환경에 의한 주의 산만도, 문제 해결에 대한 끈기, 환경에의 일반적 민감성, 전반적인 기분 및 행실과 연관이 있다.

　　이 특징들 중 어느 것이 명백히 드러나는가를 토대로 아동의 인성은 세 가지 유형 중 하나에 속하는 것으로 분류될 수 있다. '순한' 아이(easy child)는 새로운 환경에 쉽게 적응하는 경향을 보이고, 생리적 기능이 고르며, 대체로 성격이 밝고 좋은 기분 상태에 있다. 반면에 '까다로운' 아이(difficult child)는 생리적 기능이 불규칙적이고, 새로운 상황에 부정적인 반응을 보이며, 새로운 환경이나 사람에게 적응하는 것이 느리다. 둘의 중

간쯤에 있는 '더디게 반응하는' 아이(slow-to-warm-up child)는 새로운 상황에 약간 부정적인 반응을 보이기는 하지만 후자의 유형(까다로운 아이)보다 좀 더 쉽게 적응할 수 있다. 또 이들의 신체 기능은 '순한' 아이만큼 규칙적이지는 않다.

아동의 선천적 기질은 분명 가정생활에 영향을 미칠 것이다. '순한' 아이는 가정생활과 일상생활에 보다 쉽게 적응할 것이며, 이 때문에 가족 구성원들에게 부가적인 스트레스를 줄 가능성을 줄여 준다. 보다 까다로운 아이들은 특히 다른 가족 구성원들도 까다로운 성격일 경우, 이미 상당히 불안정할지도 모르는 가족간의 역학관계를 망쳐 그들 자신과 부모 및 형제 간에 보다 심한 긴장 상태를 유발할 가능성이 있다.

부모는 자녀들의 기질을 단순히 이론적인 사용으로서가 아니라 개인 및 가족 구성원 모두로서 그들을 보다 잘 이해하기 위한 수단으로서 분석해야 한다. 자녀들의 타고난 특징을 인식함으로써 부모는 긍정적인 방향으로 그들에게 대응할 수 있고, 그저 그들에게 변하기를 강요하기보다는 그들의 개인적인 성장에 영향을 미치려고 노력할 수 있다. 이것은 자녀들이 사회적으로 용인되는 방법으로 남을 대하는 법을 배우고 가정 내에서 마찰을 덜 일으키도록 도울 것이다.

구문 해설

14행 (Being) Based upon [which of these traits are manifest], a child's personality can ...
▶ [ ]는 간접의문으로 upon의 목적절이다.

19행 Somewhere in-between is the "slow-to-warm-up" child [who has ... type].
부사구 / V / S
▶ 부사구가 강조되어 문장 앞으로 나오면서 주어와 동사의 순서가 도치된 문장이다.

28행 Parents should analyze ..., **not** simply as an academic exercise, **but** *as* a means ...
▶ not A but B는 'A가 아니라 B'의 의미로 A와 B자리에 as구가 대등하게 연결되어 있다.

READING 2 TOEFL p. 58~59

정답

1. ⓑ 2. ⓓ 3. The first square 4. ⓒ 5. ⓒ
6. ⓑ, ⓒ, ⓕ

해석

몬테소리 교수법

이탈리아에서 의사 자격을 취득한 최초의 여성인 Maria Montessori 박사(1870-1952)는 아동 질병에 대한 연구를 통해 아동 발달에 관심을 갖게 되었다. 시간이 흐르면서 그녀는 교육이 불가능한 것으로 여겨지는 아동들에 대해 특별한 관심을 쏟았다. 그런 아동들에 대한 관찰에서 더 나아가 그녀는 저소득층 학생들의 교육을 위해 몬테소리 방법을 창안했다. 몬테소리의 견해는 18세기 철학자 Jean-Jacques Rousseau의 영향을 강하

게 받았는데, 그는 대작인 〈에밀〉에서 교육에 대한 자신의 견해를 제시했다. 몬테소리 방법은 나중에 전통적인 교육 기법에 대한 유명한 대안이 되었다.

몬테소리 교수법의 목표는 학생들에게 자극적인 환경을 제공하는 것이다. Montessori 박사의 학습 원칙 중 하나는 '감각 교육의 선행, 지능 교육의 후행'이었다. 그런 만큼 몬테소리 교실은 활동들과 교구들이 학습과정에서 모든 감각을 사용하게끔 고안되어 있기 때문에 '개인이 적극 참여하는' 학습 방법을 정확하게 반영한다.

초기 단계에서 학생들은 출생부터 6세까지와 6세부터 12세까지의 두 나이 집단으로 나뉜다. 이보다 더 나이가 많은 학생들을 위한 몬테소리 학교는 그렇게 널리 퍼져 있지는 않지만 존재하기는 한다. 첫 번째 단계는 '어린이들의 집'이라고 불리며 개별 학습과 학습자의 속도에 맞춘 발달에 초점을 둔다. 두 번째 단계에서 학생들은 '우주 교육'을 받는데, 이때는 타인과의 협력이 발달의 일부분으로 장려된다. 몬테소리 교실은 전통적인 학교 제도에서 대세인 교사 중심의 방법이라기보다 학생 중심이기 때문에 각 학생들이 개성있게 성장하도록 장려한다.

학생들이 하는 모든 활동에는 필요한 것이 다 갖추어져 있어서, 마치고 나면 새로운 이해 단계에 이르게 된다. 비록 활동들이 차례대로 진행되기는 하지만 언제 과제가 끝나야 하는지에 관한 규정된 시간표가 없다. 〈에밀〉의 교사와 아주 흡사한 몬테소리 교사는 학생들을 가르치기보다는 관찰을 하며 적절한 때에 그들에게 적절한 수업을 제공한다.

몬테소리 방법에 반대하는 많은 비판들이 제기되어 왔다. 일부는 차례대로 진행되는 학습 활동들이 아동의 창의성을 북돋아 주기보다는 저해한다고 믿는다. 또 다른 일부는 몬테소리 교실에서 사용되는 교수 방법론과 학습 자료들로 인해 곤란할 것이라는 이유로 몬테소리 학생들에게 숙제가 거의 주어지지 않는다는 사실을 비난한다. 그러나 그렇게 비판하는 사람들이 있음에도 불구하고 창안자의 사망 후 반세기가 지났지만 몬테소리 학교는 여전히 특정 집단에게 인기가 있다.

구문 해설

3행 ..., she ... in children [(who were) deemed (to be) unable to be educated].

17행 ... "cosmic education," **in which** collaboration with others ...
▶ in which 이하는 계속적 용법으로 쓰인 〈전치사 + 관계대명사절〉로, 앞에서부터 순차적으로 해석하는 것이 자연스럽다.

22행 ..., there is no prescribed timetable **as to** *when* tasks should be finished.
▶ as to는 '~에 관한'의 의미이고, when 이하는 간접의문으로 as to의 목적절이다.

28행 Others find fault with the fact [that Montessori pupils are ... **as** it would be ... in class].
▶ 이때의 as는 이유의 접속사로 '~이기 때문에'의 의미이다.

1. b　2. c　3. a　4. b　5. c　6. a　7. b　8. d
9. executed　10. subsequent　11. omen
12. perpetrated　13. instinctive　14. prop
15. persistence　16. dissonance　17. b　18. b
19. d　20. b　21. c　22. a　23. collaboration
24. predisposition　25. temper　26. a. 2 b. 3

UNIT 13.
Chemistry

READING 1　　　　　　　　　　　　　p. 62~63

WORD CHECK

1. pay off　2. render　3. glow　4. accelerate
▶ compound: sth made of two or more parts, especially chemical substances

정답

1. c　2. b　3. It acts to accelerate an oxidized chemical reaction between the hydrogen peroxide and luminol.　4. c　5. d　6. glow, iron, excess, destroy

해석

　　이것의 화학명은 $C_8H_7N_3O_2$이다. 자연 상태일 때, 이것은 특별할 것 없는 노르스름한 결정체이다. 그러나 과산화수소와 같은 적절한 산화제와 혼합되면 이것은 아주 특별해진다. 이것은 범죄 현장에서 빛을 내어 그렇지 않으면 육안으로는 보이지 않을 증거를 드러나게 한다.

　　'루미놀'이라고 알려진 이 화합물은 촉매에 의해 활성화될 경우 특정 색깔로 빛을 낼 것이다. 루미놀은 특정 페인트, 화학제품, 식물, 그리고 가장 중요하게는 철분이 있을 때 밝은 청록색 빛을 띤다. 혈액에는 약간의 철분이 들어 있기 때문에 루미놀은 수사관들이 심지어 혈흔이 깨끗이 씻기었거나 범죄 현장에 수년간 그대로 남아 있을 때라도 혈흔을 찾아낼 수 있게 해준다. 어두운 방에서 의심스런 부분에 루미놀을 뿌리면, 혈흔이 있을 경우 그것은 청록색 빛을 낼 것이다.

　　이 현상 이면에 있는 화학적 작용은 꽤 간단하다. 철분은 과산화수소와 루미놀 간의 화학적 산화 반응을 가속화시키는 역할을 한다. 이 반응 과정에서 루미놀은 수소와 질소 원자를 잃는 반면 산소 원자를 얻어 아주 높은 에너지 상태의 새로운 화학적 화합물이 된다. 그러나 이렇게 높은 에너지 상태의 원자 대부분은 도중에 여분의 에너지를 방출하면서 거의 즉각적으로 이전의 상태로 되돌아간다. 따라서, 루미놀의 경우 산소 원자 속의 전

자는 보다 낮은 에너지 수준으로 되돌아가며 청록색 빛으로 여분의 에너지를 방출한다.

　　사람들은 루미놀이 폭력 범죄 수사 시 일상적으로 사용될 것이라고 생각할 것이다. 그러나 실제로 그것은 주로 다른 수사 방법들이 고갈되었을 때 사용된다. 그 이유는 루미놀이 그것이 닿은 유전자 물질을 파괴하기 때문이다. 미세한 혈흔조차 탐지할 수 있는 그것의 가장 커다란 강점이 모순되게도 수사관들에게 가장 커다란 위험이 되고 있다. 이러한 혈액 샘플들은 애초에 너무 소량이기 때문에 거기에 루미놀을 뿌리는 것은 그것들을 법의학적 증거로서 무용지물이 되게 할 수 있다. 그러나 수사관들이 스스로 혈흔의 증거를 발견하지 못할 경우, 그들은 루미놀 도박이 유용한 샘플을 제공해줌으로써 성과를 거두기를 바란다.

구문 해설

[2행] ..., **when** (it is) **mixed** with an appropriate oxidant ..., it becomes *anything but* ordinary.
　▶ 부사절의 〈주어 + be동사〉는 주절의 주어와 같을 때 종종 생략한다.
　▶ anything but ~: 전혀 ~이 아닌

[5행] (Being) **Known** as "luminol," this compound will glow a certain color when (it is) activated by ...
　▶ 앞에 Being이 생략된 Known ... "luminol."은 주어 this compound를 설명하는 분사구문이다.

[13행] ..., the luminol loses hydrogen ..., **resulting in** a new chemical compound [in a ...].
　▶ resulting in 이하는 결과를 나타내는 분사구문이다.

[23행] Its greatest asset [— being able to detect ...] is, (S)　　　　　　　　　　　　　　　　　(V)
ironically, its greatest risk to investigators.　　　　　　　　　(C)

READING 2　　　　　　　　　　　　　p. 64~65

WORD CHECK

1. hamper　2. shrinkage　3. probe　4. insulate
▶ plunge: to suddenly move sth downward

정답

1. c　2. the liquid inside of a jar with gas without causing any shrinkage　3. d　4. d　5. a　6. replace, strong, air, insulating

해석

　　만일 당신이 흰색 장갑을 끼고 손을 검정색 잉크통에 집어넣으면, 당신은 당연히 그 결과가 젖은 검정색 장갑이 될 것이라고 예상할 것이다. 그러나 냉동 연기로 알려진 색다른 인공 물질로 먼저 손을 감싸면 어떻게 될까? 물기 없는 손과 흰색 장갑 그대로일 것이다.

　　냉동 연기의 정식 명칭은 '에어로젤'로, 1931년 병에 든 액체를 양의

감소 없이 기체로 대체시키겠다는 내기에서 이기려는 시도 중에 Steven Kistler에 의해 만들어졌다. Kistler는 내기에서 이겼고, 그 과정에서 에어로젤을 발견했다. 그러나 이 물질이 필요로 하는 값비싸고 어려운 제조 과정과 더불어 이 물질의 부서지기 쉬운 성질은 최근까지 광범위한 생산을 어렵게 했다.

에어로젤은 반투명의 푸르스름한 백색을 띄며 만지면 물기가 없고 거품과 비슷한 감촉이 난다. 그것은 구조적으로 극도의 다공성을 띠는데, 이는 에어로젤이 작은 구멍들로 가득 차 있다는 것을 의미한다. 이런 이유로 그것은 믿을 수 없을 정도로 가벼워서, 사람 크기 정도의 에어로젤 뭉치를 들어 올리려고 할 경우 그것의 무게가 1파운드도 안된다는 것을 알게 될 것이다. 이러한 사실에도 불구하고, 그것은 충분한 압력이 가해지면 유리처럼 산산 조각이 나기는 하지만 자신의 무게의 2,000배 이상을 지탱할 만큼 충분히 강하다.

에어로젤은 고체 물질이기는 하지만 최대 99.8%가 공기로 이루어져 있다. 그것은 겔에서 액체를 제거하고 이를 기체로 대체함으로써 다양한 화학물질들로부터 생산될 수 있다. 상업적으로 말하자면, 에어로젤의 가장 두드러진 특징은 절연 능력이다. 에어로젤은 소리와 전기를 차단하는 데 효과적이지만, 그것의 단열성이 가장 응용 가능성이 크다.

그것은 화성으로 보내진 로봇 탐사선인 Rover의 단열재로 이미 사용되었다. 그 임무 기간 동안 화성의 기온은 최저 섭씨 영하 67도까지 내려갔었지만, 에어로젤은 Rover의 내부에 있는 민감한 전자 부품들이 얼지 않고 제 기능을 수행하도록 유지시켜 주었다. 에어로젤의 또 다른 잠재 용도는 창문의 유리 대체물로서이다. 일반 유리 단열 능력의 20배를 가지고 있기 때문에, 에어로젤 창은 열 손실을 최소화하여 집주인들이 돈을 절약할 수 있도록 한다. 에어로젤은 또한 다양한 다른 방법들로도 사용될 수 있어서 진정한 다용도 물질이 되고 있다.

구문 해설

1행 If you **were to** put on a white glove …, you'd naturally **expect** the result to be …

▶ 가정법 과거 구문의 if절에 쓰인 were to-v는 미래에 실현가능성이 희박할 때 쓴다.

13행 …, with a texture [similar to **that** of foam].

▶ that은 a texture의 중복을 피하기 위해 사용한 지시대명사이다.

17행 …, it is strong enough to hold **more than 2,000 times its own weight**, …

▶ (more than) + 배수 + 명사구: ~의 몇 배 (이상)

UNIT 14.
Biology

WORD CHECK

1. mimicry　2. herd　3. predator　4. camouflage

▶ hinge on: to completely depend on

정답

1. a　2. d　3. (They scare away predators) With a pattern on their back that resembles a snake's head
4. b　5. b　6. b. blend into an environment　c. how physiology affects methods of camouflage
d. mimicking other animals　e. the role of evolution

해석

야생에서의 생존은 눈에 보이지 않게 존재하는 능력 여하에 달려 있을 수 있다. 많은 종류의 동물들은 그 목적이 포식동물로부터 스스로를 숨기는 것이든, 먹이에게 몰래 다가가는 것이든 위장을 통해 이를 달성한다. 어떤 경우이든 간에 이러한 잠복의 효과는 흔히 자연 서식지에 동화될 수 있는 동물의 능력에 기반한 것이다.

동화는 주변 환경을 닮은 색을 취함으로써 이루어질 수 있다. 예를 들어, 사슴은 주변 땅 색깔인 적갈색인 반면 상어는 바다 빛깔과 일치하는 청회색이다. 또 어떤 동물들은 환경 속이나 동일 종의 거대한 무리 사이에 스스로를 숨기기 위해 무늬나 문양을 이용한다. 예를 들어, 호랑이는 먹이를 찾아 돌아다니는 높은 풀숲에 동화되도록 줄무늬가 나 있다. 그러나 얼룩말의 줄무늬는 아주 다르게 작용한다. 얼룩말이 떼를 지어 모여 있을 때 그들의 흑백 줄무늬는 시각적 혼란을 일으키는 역할을 한다. 즉, 흑백 줄무늬는 많은 얼룩말 중에서 포식동물이 하나를 골라내는 일을 아주 어렵게 만든다.

동물들이 자신의 색깔을 환경에 맞게 변화시키는 방법은 생리 기능에 따라 다르다. 조류와 포유동물들은 일반적으로 털이나 깃털로 뒤덮여 있어서, 색깔을 변화시킬 수 없으므로 새로운 외피를 자라게 할 필요가 있다. 반면, 어떤 종들은 색소 세포로 알려진 천연색을 결정하는 세포를 통해 자신의 피부 외양을 바꿀 수 있다. 예를 들어, 갑오징어는 색과 무늬를 바꾸기 위해 피부 세포를 조작하며, 바다 달팽이는 먹이를 바꿈으로써 환경과 일치하도록 색을 바꾼다.

또 다른 유형의 위장은 모방으로 알려져 있다. 일부 곤충의 종은 생명이 없는 물체나 심지어 다른 종류의 동물인 것처럼 보이기 위해서 모방을 이용한다. 예를 들어, 포식동물이 접근해 오면 대벌레는 움직이지 않고 가만히 있어서 종종 나뭇가지로 오인된다. 그리고 박각시나방 애벌레는 뱀의 머리를 닮은 등의 무늬로 포식동물들을 쫓아버린다. 애벌레를 먹고 싶어할지도 모르는 포식동물은 아마도 뱀을 공격하지는 않을 것이다. 이러한 각각의 위장 장치는 자연 선택의 과정을 통해 서서히 발달되었다. 그 종의 다른 구성원들보다 찾아내기가 더 어려운 동물은 생존 가능성이 더 많으며,

따라서 번식을 하고 자신의 유전자를 확실히 다음 세대에게 물려줄 수 있는 기회를 갖게 된다.

구문 해설

9행 Tigers, ..., are striped **so as to** blend into the tall grasslands [(that) they roam ...].

▶ so as to-v: ~하도록, ~하기 위하여

▶ [ ]는 grasslands를 수식하는 목적격 관계대명사절이다.

12행 ..., they make **it** very difficult *for a predator* **to single out** one animal among many (animals).

▶ it은 to single out 이하의 진목적어를 가리키는 가목적어이고, a predator는 to single out 이하의 의미상의 주어이다.

READING 2   TOEFL   p. 68~69

정답

1. ⓑ 2. ⓒ 3. ⓓ 4. The second square 5. ⓑ
6. ⓑ, ⓓ, ⓔ

해석

파리지옥

파리지옥은 미국 남동부의 습지에서만 자라는 작은 식충 식물이다. 로마의 사랑의 여신을 가리키는 것으로 여겨지는 이 식물의 기이한 이름은 곤충을 잡는 이 식물의 능력을 남자를 유혹하는 아름다운 여인의 능력에 비유했던 식물학자들에 의해 선정되었다.

사실 식물학계에서 파리지옥을 눈에 띄게 하는 것은 바로 그것의 포식성이다. 비록 이 식물이 광합성을 통해 포도당을 합성할 수 있기는 하지만, 이것이 자라는 습지 토양에는 질소와 같은 다른 필수 영양소들이 부족하다. 파리지옥은 이러한 결핍을 곤충과 거미 같은 살아 있는 먹이를 섭취함으로써 보충한다.

파리지옥은 대부분의 육식동물들처럼 뇌와 근육을 갖고 있지 않기 때문에 기계적이고 화학적인 일련의 과정에 의존한다. 이 식물은 달콤한 향기가 나는 과즙을 사용하여 벌린 입처럼 생긴 특별한 형태의 잎인 그들의 덫으로 먹이를 유인한다. 이 잎은 민감한 '감각모(感覺毛)'로 덮여 있다. 곤충이 감각모 중 하나를 건드리면 이 식물은 곤충의 존재에 경계 태세를 취한다. 만일 감각모를 연달아 두 번째로 건드리면, 잎이 일부분 닫히면서 반응을 하는데, 서로 맞물려 우리를 형성하는 뻣뻣한 돌기들로 그 곤충을 가둔다.

그러나 덫은 감각모가 다시 반응하지 않는다면 완전히 닫히지 않을 것이다. 이런 방식으로 이 식물은 살아 있는 먹이와 잎에 우연히 떨어지지도 모르는 기타 물체들을 구별한다. 예를 들어, 생명이 없는 나뭇가지나 잎은 감각모를 다시 움직이게 하지 않을 것이다. 만일 감각모가 다시 반응하지 않으면 잎은 다시 서서히 열리는데, 약 12시간이 걸리는 작용이며, 불필요한 물체가 자유롭게 떨어져 나가게 해준다. 이 과정은 그 식물이 먹을 수 없는 것을 소화시키려고 하면서 귀중한 에너지를 낭비하는 일을 피하기 위한 것이다.

일단 잎이 완전히 닫혀 곤충을 내부에 가두면, 이 식물은 동물 위 속의 소화액처럼 작용을 하는 산성액을 만들어 먹이를 먹기 시작한다. 먹이는 다음 며칠 간의 기간에 걸쳐 서서히 용해되고 영양소는 식물에 의해 흡수된다. 영양소가 다 섭취되면 덫이 다시 열리고 찌꺼기가 떨어져 나간다. 그 다음에 의심을 하지 않는 생물이 우연히 덫에 걸리면 이 과정은 다시 시작될 것이다.

구문 해설

2행 The plant's odd name, [thought to be ... love], was chosen by botanists [who **compared** the plant's ability ... **to** a beautiful woman's ability ...].

▶ 첫 번째 [ ]는 The plant's odd name을 수식하는 과거분사구이다.

▶ compare A to B: A를 B에 비유하다

5행 **It is**, in fact, the Venus flytrap's predatory nature **that** makes it stand out ...

▶ It is ~ that ... 강조구문으로 the Venus flytrap's predatory nature를 강조하고 있다.

10행 The plants attract their prey into their traps – specially formed leaves [that resemble ... mouth] ...

▶ specially formed leaves는 their traps를 부연설명하는 동격 어구이다.

14행 ..., the leaf responds ..., **trapping** the insect with stiff protuberances [that interlock to form a cage].

▶ trapping 이하는 동시동작을 나타내는 분사구문이다.

UNIT 15.
Politics

READING 1   p. 70~71

WORD CHECK

1. critical   2. impartiality   3. coverage   4. liaison
▶ avenue: a means of doing sth

정답

1. d   2. (They maintain their impartiality) By operating independently outside of the system   3. c   4. c   5. d
6. a. the background b. the political role c. the duties of organizational ombudsmen d. how news ombudsmen operate e. the value of ombudsmen

옴부즈맨은 불만 사항을 받고 조사함으로써 대중과 조직 사이에서 연락자 역할을 하는 관리이다. 이상하게 들리는 이 명칭은 스웨덴어에서 유래하지만 표준 영어로 사용되어 왔다. 비록 전 세계 여러 문화권에서 유사한 직책들이 존재하기는 했지만 근대 최초의 공식적 옴부즈맨은 19세기 초 스웨덴 정부에 의해 임명되었다.

옴부즈맨은 선출된 관리들에 대해 불만이 있는 일반 시민들의 대표자 역할을 하면서 전통적으로 정치적 역할을 수행한다. 비록 옴부즈맨은 국민들에 의해 선출되는 것과 반대로 정부에 의해 임명될지라도 그들은 조직 외부에서 독자적으로 활동함으로써 그들의 공정성을 유지한다. 그들은 일반적으로 부정 행위의 증거가 발견될지라도 정부에 대해 법적 조치를 취할 권한은 없지만, 그들의 발견에 대한 보고를 공포함으로써 그 상황을 조사에 착수시킬 수 있다. 가능한 한 그들은 법정으로까지 가기 전에 상황을 해결하려고 노력한다.

그러나 오늘날 옴부즈맨의 지위는 대학, 사기업, 병원, 비영리단체와 같은 다양한 비정부 기관에서도 활용되고 있다. 기관 옴부즈맨은 공정함을 유지하는 것이 중요하다. 그들은 주로 회사 직원의 법적, 윤리적 이익을 보호할 책임이 있다. 그들은 또한 그들의 고용주에게 영향을 미칠 수도 있는 새로운 문제들을 감시하여, 문제를 일으키기 전에 이를 처리한다. 기관 옴부즈맨은 고위 관리이지만 회사 경영진의 일부는 아니며, 종종 이사진에게 보고를 한다.

뉴스 옴부즈맨은 또 다른 형태의 비정부 지위로 주로 매체에 의해 고용된다. 이 지위는 대중들에게 그들의 불만을 토로하는 통로를 제공해 주며 언론인들이 대중의 의견을 계속 접할 수 있게 해준다. 뉴스 옴부즈맨은 보도 기사들의 정확성과 공정성에 대한 불만을 경청하고 나서 관련된 언론인과 편집자에게 제안을 한다. 그렇게 함으로써, 그들은 독자들이나 시청자들이 발언권을 가질 수 있게 그들을 장려하는 한편 앞으로의 뉴스 보도가 공정하고 균형을 유지할 수 있도록 보장한다.

국민들에게 그들의 불만을 들어주는 귀뿐만이 아니라 목소리도 제공하면서, 옴부즈맨이 대중을 다루는 어떤 종류의 기관에서든지 중요한 역할을 할 수 있다는 사실은 점점 더 분명해지고 있다.

구문 해설

13행 They generally don't have the power [to take ...] if evidence of wrongdoing is found ...
▶ if는 양보를 나타내는 접속사로 '비록 ~하더라도'의 의미이다.

21행 They also monitor new issues [that may ... employers], **addressing** them ...
▶ addressing 이하는 연속동작을 나타내는 분사구문이다.

31행 **It** has become increasingly apparent **that** ombudsmen can play ... role in any sort of organization [that deals with the public], *providing* citizens ...
▶ It은 가주어이고 that ... public이 진주어이다.
▶ providing 이하는 동시동작을 나타내는 분사구문이다.

WORD CHECK

1. prioritize　2. rhetoric　3. paternalistic
4. reformative
▶ charitable: generous with one's time, money, belongings, etc.

정답

1. c　2. Argentina fell deep into debt and faced abrupt economic ruin.　3. b　4. b　5. a. the origin of populism b. how populism damaged Argentina c. the features of populist policies d. the effect of populism on an economy

해석

대중주의(populism)는 일반적으로 대중의 이익을 향상시키는 것을 주장하는 정치적 활동이나 이상을 말한다. 종종 대중주의는 권력을 얻거나 유지하기 위한 수단으로서, 대중의 이익을 유리하게 이용하는 정당의 전략으로 이해된다. 대중주의라는 용어는 1891년에 미국에서 처음 조직된 파퓰리스트당 혹은 인민당에서 유래했다. 그것은 다른 정당들과 경쟁하기 위해서 대중에게 호소하는 정책을 내놓았다. 이 전략은 후에 대중주의의 전형적인 특징으로 알려지게 되었다.

아르헨티나의 전 대통령 부부인 Juan Peron과 Eva Peron은 대중주의정치가의 잘 알려진 예이다. 2차 세계 대전 후 대중의 지지에 힘입어 대통령에 선출된 Juan Peron은 자신의 권력을 유지하기 위해 친노동 정책을 채택했다. 그는 또한 대중에게 무제한의 물질적 지원을 제공하여 자신의 정책을 개혁적인 것으로 정당화했다. 한편 그의 아내 Eva Peron은 '아르헨티나의 어머니'로 존경받았다. 그녀는 부자들에게는 냉담하게 대했고 가난한 사람들에게는 친절하고 관대했다. 그러나 그들의 급진적인 개혁의 결과로 아르헨티나는 심한 부채에 빠졌고 갑작스런 경제 위기에 직면했다. 1940년대까지 세계 5대 경제 강국의 하나였던 아르헨티나는 오늘날에도 여전히 대중주의의 결과로 어려움을 겪고 있다.

대중주의 정책들 이면에는 항상 대중의 지지를 얻으려는 의도가 있다. 대중주의정치인들은 종종 대중과 직접적인 대화를 갖고 그들의 생각을 글로 표현함으로써 온정적인 태도를 취한다. 그들은 또한 부자들과 권력자들의 특권을 비난하며, 한편으로는 그들의 반엘리트 사상으로 중산층과 하류층에게 호소한다. 그것이 바로 그들이 종종 부의 분배를 우선하는 정책을 쓰는 이유이다.

얼핏 보면 대중들에게 이익이 되는 것처럼 보이기 때문에 대중주의정책에는 잘못된 것이 없는 것처럼 보인다. 그러나 지나친 부의 분배를 요구하는 정책은 엄청난 재정적 손실과 인플레이션을 일으킬 수 있다. 이는 저성장이라는 악순환에 이르게 하여, 대중에게 저임금을 안겨주고 궁극적으로는 국가 경제를 위협한다.

전 세계적으로 많은 정치인들은 지지를 얻기 위해 여전히 대중주의 정서에 의존하고 있다. 바라건대, 그런 언변 이면에 정책에 대한 대중의 지지를 정치적 권력을 잡기 위한 수단으로 사용되게 하는 것이 아니라, 국가 성장을 위한 초석이 되도록 하는 지혜가 있었으면 한다.

구문 해설

17행 **Having been** a top five world economic power ...
1940s, Argentina is still struggling ...
▶ Having ... 1940s는 완료형 분사구문으로 주절보다 앞선 때를 나타내며, Although Argentina was a top ... 1940s의 의미를 지닌다.

26행
This leads to ...
　　causing lower wages for the public
　　and
low growth,　**ultimately threatening** the national economy.
▶ causing ... public과 ultimately threatening 이하는 둘 다 결과를 나타내는 분사구문이다.

30행 ..., behind the rhetoric lies the wisdom [to turn
　　　　　　　　　부사구　　　V　　S
popular support for policies ...], instead of allowing
it to be utilized as a means ...
▶ it은 popular support for policies를 가리킨다.

UNIT 16.
Law

READING 1　　　　　　　　　　　　p. 74~75

WORD CHECK

1. offense　2. expiration　3. irrelevance　4. lawsuit
▶ perpetrator: one who has done sth wrong or committed a crime

정답

1. b　2. c　3. c　4. It's because it may encourage criminal behavior.　5. c　6. responsible, fairness, techniques, unsolvable

해석

이상적인 법치 체제에서는 모든 범죄자들은 재판에 즉시 회부되어 범죄에 대해 처벌을 받을 것이다. 그러나 실제로는 일단 특정 기간이 경과되면 범죄자들을 범죄로 인해 재판에 회부되는 부담에서 벗어나게 하는 법이 있다. 그 기원이 로마 시대로 거슬러 올라가는 이 법은 '공소시효(출소기한 법)'로 알려져 있다.

공소시효에 의해 정해진 만료기간은 소송 사건의 유형에 따라 다르며 그러한 법령이 적용되지 않는 일부 소송 사건의 유형들도 있다. 미국 대부분의 주에서는 살인 사건에 대한 공소시효가 없으며, 살인 용의자에 대해 소송을 제기할 수 있는 권리에 대한 공소 시한도 전혀 없다. 그러나 많은 국가에서 공소시효는 심지어 살인 사건에도 적용된다. 나라마다 살인에 대한 만료기간을 서로 다르게 정해 놓고 있는데, 예를 들어 한국은 25년이

고 대만은 30년이다.

공소시효를 지지하는 사람들은 입법자들이 이 법을 제정한 데에는 타당한 이유가 있다고 주장한다. 공소시효의 한 가지 목적은 공정성을 유지하는 것이다. 다시 말해서, 시간이 경과함에 따라 기억들은 사라지고 증거는 손상될 수 있으며 목격자가 사라져서 정황들이 법정 재판에 부적합해 질 수 있다. 공소시효를 지지하는 또 다른 이유는 종결 혹은 확실성으로, 사회와 법 집행기관들이 결국 해결될 것 같지 않은 오래된 사건들을 조사하는 데 노력과 공공 자원을 들이는 것을 멈추고, 대신 그들의 관심을 최근 범죄로 돌리는 것을 의미한다.

공소시효를 반대하는 사람들은 그것을 부적절한 것으로 보며, 법제도가 시대에 맞게 갱신되어야 한다고 주장한다. 그들은 첫째로 과학 수사에서의 진보를 지적한다. 증거 복원과 분석에 사용되는 현대 기술들은 범죄가 행해진지 한참 뒤에도 증명될 수 있다는 것을 의미한다. 둘째로 그들은 특정 범죄들이 절대로 미결사건 파일로 분류되어서는 안 되며, 범인들은 반드시 자신의 죄에 대한 대가를 치러야 한다고 믿는다. 그들은 살인범이나 아동 성폭행범들이 처벌받지 않고 달아나게 두는 것은 그런 범죄 행위를 조장하는 것일 수도 있다고 주장한다.

법적으로 정당하든 도덕적으로 정당하든 간에 공소시효는 적어도 사회적 관심을 반영해야만 한다. 입법자들은 처벌이 사회 질서의 도구이기도 하지만 법에 대한 신뢰 역시 그렇다는 사실을 반드시 유념해야 한다.

구문 해설

3행 ..., there are laws [that actually free criminals from
the burden **of** being brought to court for their crimes
once a certain amount of time has passed].
▶ of: 동격의 전치사
▶ once는 접속사로 '일단 ~하면'의 의미이다.

17행 Another reason ...　is eventually stop investing ...,
..., **meaning** (that)　and
society ... will　instead turn their attention ...
▶ meaning 이하는 부연설명의 분사구문이다.

29행 Lawmakers must remain mindful of the fact [**that**
punishment is a tool of social order], but **that** *so too
is faith in the law*].
▶ 2개의 that절이 등위접속사에 의해 이어질 때 두 번째 that은 생략되지 않는다.
▶ so too is faith in the law는 faith in the law is a tool of social order가 축약 및 도치된 구문이다.

READING 2　TOEFL　　　　　　　p. 76~77

정답

1. ⓒ　2. ⓑ　3. ⓐ　4. The second square　5. ⓐ
6. ⓒ, ⓔ, ⓕ

배심원 재판

전 세계의 여러 국가에서처럼 미국에서도 기소된 범죄자들은 배심원 제도 하에서 재판을 받는다. 일반인으로 구성된 배심원단은 소송 사건에서 사실들을 심리하고 평결을 내리는 일을 부여받는다. 판사가 모든 적법한 법률들과 행동 지침들이 잘 준수되도록 하기 위해 재판을 주재하지만 배심원의 결정에는 간섭하지 않는다. 이러한 개념의 여러 가지 형태가 고대 이후로 실행되어 왔지만, 현대 배심원 제도의 초기 형태는 일부 국민들에게 동료 집단 앞에서 재판을 받을 수 있는 권리를 허용하는 영국 문서인 〈마그나 카르타〉에 의해 도입되었다.

배심원단은 대부분의 경우 12명에 이르는 각각의 배심원들로 구성된다. 배심원들은 피고측과 기소자측 모두에 의해 제시되는 증언과 주장을 듣고 이러한 사실들을 고려해서 유죄 또는 무죄 평결을 내린다. 단순한 과반수에서부터 배심원단의 만장일치에 이르기까지, 상황에 따라 평결을 내리는데 요구되는 조건들이 다르다.

미국의 배심원들은 등록된 유권자와 면허가 있는 운전자 목록에서 무작위로 선발된다. 그러나 많은 사람들이 배심원 자격에서 제외되는데, 배심원단으로 봉사할 시간을 낼 수 없는 직업의 사람들과 질병, 범죄 기록, 상충되는 종교적 믿음을 가진 사람들이다. 예비 배심원들은 또한 피고측과 기소자측에 의해 인정되기에 앞서 소송 사건에 있어서 편견이나 외부적 이해관계가 없음을 증명하기 위해 조사를 받아야 한다.

재판 기간 동안 배심원들은 재판 장소 밖에서 소송 사건에 대한 어떤 정보의 입수도 금지되어 있다. 이것은 그들로 하여금 피고측과 기소자측에 의해 제시된 사실들에만 집중하게 한다. 일단 재판이 끝나면 배심원단은 소송 사건에 대한 평결을 심의하기 위해 모인다. 심의에 대해 정해진 기한은 없으며, 미국의 형사 재판은 만장일치의 판결을 요구해서 배심원단이 평결을 내리는 데 며칠이 걸리는 것으로 알려져 있다.

배심원 제도는 일반인이 법의 집행에 참여할 수 있도록 허용하기 때문에 민주주의 정부의 필수 요소로 보인다. 선발 과정이 무작위이기 때문에 배심원들은 지역 인구의 다양하고 정확한 표본을 나타낸다. 이런 식으로 하여 형사 재판 제도는 지역사회의 우위에 있거나 지역사회와 대립하지 않고 긴밀하게 연계되어 있다.

구문 해설

6행 ... was introduced by the Magna Carta, an English document [**granting** certain people the right ...].

▶ granting 이하는 an English document를 수식하는 현재분사구이다.

8행

The jurors
- listen to the testimonies and arguments [presented by ... prosecution],
- consider these facts,
- and
- agree on a verdict of ...

14행 However, many people are ... **those** *whose* jobs ... and people with medical conditions, ...

▶ those는 people을 가리키는 지시대명사이고, whose는 those를 선행사로 하는 소유격 관계대명사이다.

WORD REVIEW TEST

UNIT 13~16   p. 78-79

1. a   2. d   3. c   4. d   5. a   6. c   7. b
8. hampered   9. deliberating   10. insulated
11. disguised   12. manipulate   13. porous
14. deficiency   15. unanimous   16. inedible   17. d
18. b   19. a   20. a   21. d   22. a   23. conceal
24. trap   25. take on   26. a. 2 b. 3

ADVANCED
READING
EXPERT